Unbinding Prometheus
Education for the Coming Age

Unbinding Prometheus
Education for the Coming Age

Donald Cowan

THE DALLAS INSTITUTE PUBLICATIONS
THE DALLAS INSTITUTE OF HUMANITIES AND CULTURE
DALLAS

Cover and design by Patricia Mora and Maribeth Lipscomb

"Science, History, and the Evidence of Things Not Seen" reprinted
by permission of Harper and Row, Publishers, Inc. © 1976.

"College Education and Leadership" appeared previously as
the President's foreword to the catalog of the University of Dallas.

"Scientific Discovery and Gratitude" is used by permission
of Thanks-Giving Square, Dallas.

The Dallas Institute Publications,
formerly known as The Pegasus Foundation,
publishes works concerned with the
imaginative, mythic, and symbolic sources of culture.
The Dallas Institute of Humanities and Culture
2719 Routh Street, Dallas Texas 75201

Contents

PREFACE   vii

INTRODUCTION   *Between Two Ages*   1

Cultural Myths

1   The New Age: Unbinding Prometheus   21
2   A Spectre of the Past: Renouncing Faust   33
3   The Perennial Future: Learning with Prospero   50

Education

4   The Spirit of Liberal Learning   71
5   The Three Moments of Learning   84
6   Universal Liberal Education   93
7   Imagination, Redundancy, and the Act
     of Learning   104
8   The Uncertainty Principle in Education   118
9   The Purpose of Educational Institutions   132
10   College Education and Leadership   143

Science, Technology, and Society

11   The Technological Imagination   149
12   The New Technology and the Polis   169
13   The Rise of the Quantitative World View   180
14   Science, History, and the Evidence of
     Things Not Seen   188
15   Scientific Discovery and Gratitude   201
16   The Economics of Taste   211

INDEX   225

Preface

EDUCATION is an enterprise that no one knows much about—
not those who manage it, those who govern it, those who
support it, nor even those who practice it. Each segment of
the total educational operation supposes for any particular
school a different though equally conventional purpose. The
reason for this diversity is simple: education is radically mis-
construed, though people have concerned themselves with its
aims and written about its purposes since the time of Plato.
The chief educational motive is the imaginative act we call
learning; the chief educational responsibility is the perpetuation and extension of culture. An understanding of these two
aspects of the educational process is doubly important in a
time of social change such as our own—a time, in fact, undergoing one of the most radical and potentially violent cultural
shifts in history. This present collection of essays is hardly
likely to avert the cultural catastrophe which it predicts or,
for that matter, to alter to any appreciable extent the current
misguided course of our schools and universities. Nonetheless, some worrying of the old verities may help to clarify our
sight and strengthen our purpose. Perhaps such concern may
shake off a bit of the dust that enshrouds education in our
day, confusing our vision and obscuring the outlines of this
primary formative action in which society is engaged.

Ours is without doubt a time in which educational reform
is widespread. The concern is nationwide and the proposed
remedies are far-ranging. Yet the locus for reform can only be
the individual school or college—its curriculum and its

teachers—two features that seem to be shuffled aside in most visions of educational improvement. It is not so much in the specifics of content that the curriculum needs to be reconceived as in its coherence and general aims. Nor is it in method and accountability that teaching should be reconstituted, but in depth and authority. The primary task of administration, therefore, is to protect faculty and curriculum against the whims of relevancy and the misapplications of efficiency. The president's (or principal's) chief responsibility is to remind his institution of its purposes and to find a way to instruct individual professors without insulting the faculty or diluting the effectiveness of other administrative officers. In the development of the ethos of a school, an important element is the influence of presidential addresses to faculty, students, academic assemblies, and civic communities. The serious administrative declaration defines and objectifies policy, placing it above argument. In such an address, something other than reiteration is needed, some new slant of light that reflects a different facet of the enterprise so that its dimensions are more fully comprehended. Avoiding accusation, a speech can suggest corrections in thought or procedure while in the process of awarding praise and recognition and can thereby discuss aims truthfully without giving offense. The speech is an accepted symbol of leadership.

As part of an occasion of celebration, a speech ought not be dispassionate. Quite properly, its motive arises from moral urgency and therefore it appropriately employs an affective language. A formal speech may indeed instruct or profess as the occasion demands, but it seeks to effect in its community of hearers a change that is primarily volitional and only incidentally logical. Though different in form and purpose from a professional paper, a speech observes fully as strict an integrity. But its argument need not be exhaustive. Rather, a speech supposes a common fund of cultural information, a common history of some extent, a shared myth, a set of legends and implicit pieties, the "old verities." It draws on that fund, sounds its numbers and sets them into resonance in a new sequence, a new rhythmic line whose original lyrics call forth an old harmony. But it avoids manipulating these resources; instead, it evokes their presence and assumes their relevance to the audience. The effect of a speech should be to call into the present a memory that the audience may not have known it held, to summon up an ideal it may not have dreamed it shared.

All celebrations are communal, and the occasion of a speech defines, in a sense, the community of the moment. An assemblage of professors that was merely a meeting while discussing professional matters or voicing dissatisfaction about parking or pay scales becomes a faculty when a speech calls its members to their disciplines. A speaker in the position of leader can bind them to their intellectual vocations and, at least momentarily, to a common purpose. I suppose what I am saying is that the speech discovers its powers in the oral tradition and thereby becomes one of the last remnants of tribal unity, one of the first seeds of *communitas*.

What is presented in this volume is basically a set of speeches, delivered over a period of fifteen years' presidency at the University of Dallas and a subsequent decade of reflection on that experience as a Fellow at the Dallas Institute of Humanities and Culture. Some of them were delivered to the faculty and student body of the Thomas More Institute in Merrimack, New Hampshire. These pieces have been edited, some of them updated but not, except in a few instances, rewritten; they no doubt contain not a little repetition and possibly some inconsistency. In going back through them, however, I was surprised to discover even in the earliest among them a theme which I have since pursued at some length and which I can now state with little fear of seeming improbable: *At the end of an era dominated by science, approaching a new epoch made possible largely by technology, we desperately need, both for the transition and the new age to come, the kind of education that for centuries has been called liberal.* It was a privilege to be able to address this topic at a fine young university and, later, among sympathetic and intelligent friends at the Dallas Institute.

The greatest privilege of the entire experience has been the corporate endeavor—now approaching its half-century mark —shared with a literary scholar, my wife. Only for half a dozen of those fifty years was our work distinct. Most of the time we strove together to discern as much as our different disciplines—literature and physics—would allow. Freely we exchanged ideas and participated in each other's writings. We could not ourselves identify what phrases of hers are in my work nor mine in hers. This acknowledgement is, then, not dutifully *pro forma* but a matter of professional integrity.

I am indebted to Gail Thomas and Robert Sardello at the Dallas Institute, who for some time have urged me to collect these speeches. The Institute has been helpful in myriad ways. I am grateful to Dona Gower and Christine Cowan for reading parts of the manuscript with care and concern. Mary Bonifield has served as production manager for this book, designing the format and performing the composition; her intelligence and patience, as well as her familiarity with the subject matter of this work, have been immense resources for my wife and me in preparing the text.

To print a speech is to commit an act of violence, to wrench a limb from a torso. The act of reading a speech properly, therefore, requires a recreation of the event by the reader, not the historical occurrence so much as an equivalent ceremonial acceptance. The language itself may accomplish this reanimation, as it does notably for some short remarks made at Gettysburg. But most speakers must seek the reader's indulgence on the occasion of printing old speeches. And so I do here.

For Louise—

in whose eyes
a brave new world is already achieved

Introduction:
Between Two Ages

THE ESSAYS THAT FOLLOW, concerned with science, technology, education, and culture, attempt to examine the relations between these communal endeavors which, in their proper exercise, offset the natural downward course of society. The idea underlying most of these pieces and more or less binding them together is that we are now between two ages, on the threshold of a new epoch in human history. A certain skepticism no doubt should greet this pronouncement. The word *new*, though much in use, is somewhat suspect. The 1987 volume of *Books in Print* lists well over a thousand titles beginning with "new." It is a fine word, obviously, burgeoning with all the "blind hopes" that, according to Aeschylus, Prometheus bequeathed to the race of men. Hence, to say that a new age is upon us ought to sound a clarion call of hope. Yet most of us tend to remain skeptical that any genuinely new and unfamiliar world could be in the making under our very noses, since we are used to seeing a new age always beginning for each of us.

To locate the genuine new, one must make a *schnitt*, a cut, in the long continuum of time, defining the instant *now*. In a continuum of numbers, if a cut is made at any specific number, mathematicians tell us, then that dividing number must be assigned to either one or the other of the two segments, not to both. And, if we are to be mathematically precise, so it is with the present moment. In the continuum of time, the present *now* must belong either to the past or to the future. For some who stand in review of time's procession, that instant represents the terminus of the past; such people look with dismay at the abyss ahead. For others, the proper children of Prometheus, this moment is the beginning of a future they see illumined in hope.

Professors who write books, whatever their political persuasion, tend to line up with the view of the present as a culmination of the past. The past is sure and certain; no probabilities exist in that golden land. Professors regard that retrospect with satisfaction; but, looking down from Olympian heights at the dubious present, they see the impious young scurrying about unpredictably, violating the niceties of the orderly past. Even the brightest among them show little interest in reclaiming the old order of things implicit in what they have been taught, preferring instead what seems to their mentors an almost perverse independence. Thus, as a recent commentator on campus life notes, the characteristic attitude of professors toward their students is always outrage. Thomas Mann has written a complex and subtle short story—"Disorder and Early Sorrow"—dealing with the tendency among academics to love not so much truth as the intellectual constructions of their own minds. In the story, Professor Cornelius is secretly aware of this weakness in himself, though he views the chaos of the present more with chagrin than outrage:

> He knows that history professors do not love history because it is something that comes to pass, but only because it is something that *has* come to pass; that they hate a revolution like the present one because they feel it is lawless, incoherent, irrelevant—in a word unhistoric; that their hearts belong to the coherent, disciplined, historic past. . . . The Past is immortalized; that is to say, it is dead; and death is the root of all godliness and all abiding significance.

There is indeed in the professorial assessment of the young, when it is spoken to the world at large, "something ulterior." Mann continues: "that something is hostility, hostility against the history of today, which is still in the making and thus not history at all, in behalf of the genuine history that has already happened—that is to say, death."

Fortunately, in the classroom itself professors tend to put aside their fear and horror at change and jump the infinitesimal gap between past and future. They become Promethean —that is to say, they become teachers. Within the sacred space of the classroom, that temple with doors closed so that learning can be celebrated, they see in those bright faces spread before them the perennial future. This vision of the "seeds of time" is the defining outlook of education.

In our own day, however, the future confronts us, not simply the normal lifespan to come, inherent in every class of young people. We encounter something radically different in almost any gathering of the young, something that challenges us with its otherness. Their music exemplifies it, their dancing, their casual dismissal of polarities—in gender, in status, in responsibility. For, without our knowing it, the world has already said farewell to an epoch of some four centuries' dynamic expansion in one basic direction. Reluctant to enter a new age, we are at risk of mindlessly insisting on preserving the patterns of the old. In particular are educators in danger of prolonging a perilously outmoded concept of education, one that continually seeks to restore the structures of an era that has passed.

It is the thesis of this book, accordingly, that an age with which we are familiar has already ended; that new forms and structures are already carrying the burden of the energies of our society; that young people sense this change in the depths of their being and are seeking ways to fulfill the new sorts of tasks to which they are called; that educational systems in our time have for the most part ignored the realities of such a change and seek only to restore the structures of a former epoch or else, with a show of ingenuity, to foster an outmoded process of analysis and innovation.

We live always in a myth—a large overarching metaphor that gives philosophical meaning to the experience of everyday life. It is difficult to see the myth one lives in; like the air, it is necessary but invisible. Yet we give that myth final secular authority. It settles our quarrels, traces out our destiny, gives form to our purpose, limits the range of our imagination. Myth is a social phenomenon, belonging to a particular people at a particular time. At birth, human beings fall into it as into a dream, as the philosopher Stein tells Marlow in *Lord Jim*. If we try to pull out of "the destructive element," we shall drown. For the myth into which we are born is more than a world view; it is an invisible extension of the very shape of life as we are given it to live at any particular period. Myth is not archetypal—the same for everyone all over the world—not coeternal with time, not sitting at the edge of reality ready to thrust into the midst of our actions the terrible contingency of the human condition. Rather, the myth of a people is a refining social thing that gives form to life, shepherding the building of a culture. Since we each live in a nest of cultures—home, school, church, city, nation—so we participate in several overlapping myths. But for most of the civilized world thus far, one perduring myth has constituted history, stretching from Greece, expanding outward, encompassing as it grows. Perhaps parochially, we call it the West. Transformations of this myth, encountering a sufficient mass of new material, have given rise to various cultural myths and by its permutations have shaped different ages of history.

The prevailing myth of the modern age has been *fact*. During the past four centuries, for Western culture—primarily Euro-American—authority has resided in a rational structure erected on facts. That is to say, the rights claimed by modernity for the necessary civilizing constructions of thought were authenticated by the facts they encompassed. This myth, which still seems to us virtually incontrovertible, began to assume its form in the early Renaissance. In it the observable objects of the world came to exist in their own right. Rather than taking their meaning from a context, a whole to which they gave up part of their very nature in order to participate in a larger reality, facts began to be considered the unchallengeable substance of life, with every larger entity becoming a kind of epi-phenomenon. Though facts might still be considered the creations of an overpower or a supreme being, still subject in principle to divine order, they nonetheless were established in a rational universe as firm pegs of meaning on which people could agree. A fact, we should remember, is a phenomenon taken as truth—a communal event, not a subjective awareness or an article of faith. And though other things—ideas and beliefs—might also be held in common by a community, these less tangible entities began to seem increasingly phantasmal while the observables, those things which are verifiable, assumed a reality not subject to bias. In this sense, facts are inherently secular, although that understanding was slow in development.

The authority that facts thus took on engendered a new concern for description with a consequent delimitation of thought—a splitting of language into denotative and connotative. Numerical language began to be thought of as the ultimate in denotation, providing a dispassionate communication. Measurement was its instrument. And, by the time of which I am speaking, the early seventeenth century, accuracy and precision of measurement had increased enormously among scientists and had begun to assume their verifying status in society at large. Precise measurements in astronomy and astrology had long been in vogue. Early in the fifteenth century a sudden burst of enthusiasm for precision had led to the invention of the decimal system. In the sixteenth century a tenfold increase in precision was accomplished by Tycho Brahe by the simple expedient of building instruments ten times larger than already existed. Scales experienced a similar increase in precision through the use of jewel bearings, and soon ingenious devices such as the vernier and the micrometer yielded precise measurements well beyond the needs of then current utility. Beginning in the fifteenth century, cartography—mapmaking—came into its great age, engendered as much by a desire for well-defined facts as by the spirit of exploration. And in a different dimension—time—clocks were developed, culminating in the pendulum of Galileo and a little later the balance-wheel watch of Huygens.

This story of one aspect of the Renaissance is, of course, familiar. I mention it here to remind ourselves that there was a time in history when facts began to assume the authority that ideas and beliefs and large purposeful structures had previously held. The perfect circles of the astronomers, to which Galileo stubbornly adhered, gave way to the ellipses of Kepler, who fitted the careful measurements of Tycho on the position of planets to their courses in time. Theory now deserted the search for an ideal realm and directed itself toward an accounting for facts. Science thus became the great allegory of facts. It found its philosopher in Descartes in his *Discourse on Method* (1637). The literary world's figure for the scientist was Francis Bacon, with his *Novum Organum* (1620). Though he contributed nothing to speak of to science, his body of work may still be taken as a clear exposition of the new mystique of the fact. Bacon believed that if one gathered all possible evidence about a phenomenon and shook it all up together, out would drop exact knowledge. He sought facts in the conviction that they were incontrovertible, able to destroy idolatrously held false knowledge.

One of Shakespeare's plays in particular, *Othello*, demonstrates the new and essentially devastating effects of a final credence given to fact. All the innuendoes and lies of a malignant Iago cannot convince Othello of his wife's infidelity until these fabrications are suddenly validated by a single fact: a handkerchief. And indeed the handkerchief that Othello gave to Desdemona is irrefutably, visibly, in Cassio's possession. The fact is certain and Desdemona is by its testimony unfaithful, even though the truth is quite otherwise, as the faithful Emilia testifies—from the heart and not simply from "evidence."

Upon reflection, we must realize that in crises we do give authority over to facts beyond their immediate demands. Facts are disparate things, occurring here and there in patterns imposed upon them. We live our lives in turmoil, in the midst of things, hurling ourselves into space and time, not aware of the "facts" of our lives any more than Molière's Monsieur Jourdain is aware that he has been speaking prose all his life—that is, until an expert tells him so. Some high priest, likewise, must make us aware of "facts," must interpret them for us. It may be an economist, a psychologist, a biologist, or some other expert who dons the guise of science. Or it could be the next level of practitioners: doctors, lawyers, financiers, and the kind of teachers who still operate on the level of lore, though in our time a lore derived from science or a scientized history. The authority of these experts does not lie so much in their own brilliance as in the guaranteed facts that support them. The journal *Science* increasingly reports retractions by scientists of conclusions reached from erroneous data, compounded of facts falsified by an assistant. As we see in these instances, when facts are in question, authority of interpretation disappears, even from a theory that seems eminently sensible and logical.

Doubt is the worm that gnaws at the myth. Of itself, uncertainty does not constitute doubt. Some imprecision in knowledge is always to be expected in any intellectual scheme; in the myth of fact such imprecision results from limitations in the instruments that determine facts and from a possible fallibility in the rational structure that interconnects them. But in principle, absolute knowledge, the goal of the Enlightenment, is possible; instruments could be perfected, logic extended, and the myth of fact remain in full authority.

But once a basic indeterminacy is discovered in knowledge itself, doubt creeps into the popular mind, which is where myth has its abiding presence. Theoretical physics, with the Uncertainty Principle and the Theory of Relativity, has shaken our faith in any absolute knowledge about space and time. The myth of fact has lost its footing.

Planck's constant (1901) designates only an insignificant amount of indeterminacy in practical applications. No bridges collapse because of it. The mechanical world is unaffected by this minute unit of uncertainty. In science, only physics (and physical chemistry) respond to its message. Not even the New Biology pays heed. Despite the small range of its influence, however, the "fact" of Planck's constant shakes the foundation of the myth of fact. Predictability loosens its grip when the precise models erected by logic are no longer infallible. Though a kind of rationality in the association of phenomena can be reestablished through other systems such as wave mechanics, the probability thus attained is not a satisfactory replacement for certainty, at least as far as the myth of fact is concerned.

Relativity (1905), though less damaging to the basis of meaning than indeterminacy, is perhaps more shattering in the popular mind. It merely introduces an observer into the knowing medium, but by so doing it destroys absolute simultaneity and even sequencing—whether A precedes B or vice versa—within a certain "light cone." Ponderable bodies, too, become variables; and mass, the very stuff of existence, is seen to be a form of energy. In relativity, the senses no longer dictate a common sense, a sense held in common by all. The consequent question becomes inevitable: "Where does truth reside?"

The decay of a myth, of course, does not *cause* an age to end in any direct way. Rather the myth's decay characterizes the decline. Ages end because the institutions society develops to express the myth are perfected to the point of exhaustion, to where the accomplishment of ends diminishes satisfaction. The "gains" made by continued innovations are negative. The old authority may sustain established institutions for a time by law or regulation, but the consequent social stagnation sets up an instability in cost against benefit, bringing into question the entire basis of the myth. A society sometimes consciously invites a kind of turmoil when it relinquishes the security provided by artificial support. The deregulation of financial institutions and airlines has recently brought this situation into stark relief; the release of instabilities occasions sufficient chaos to shake the public commitment to free enterprise. The presence of instabilities in the stock market has been dramatized by "raiders" who see the difference between the price of a stock and its actual value and capitalize on the discrepancy. But it is this very margin that has traditionally served as a collateral of extra value, assuring a good investment; when it is exploited and removed, the market has no keel to keep the financial bark steady. It is apparent by now that the concept of absentee ownership central to capitalism must undergo some fundamental changes in order to regain stability. Indeed, all the institutions of society seem to be shifting their bases, as befits the end of an era.

Coming now to a new age, can we yet discern its governing myth? Is it totally new, or more like the Renaissance was to the Middle Ages or Rome to Greece—a second try at exploring the prevailing myth? As early as 1961 Susanne Langer wrote:

> A new culture is probably in the making, which will catch up with the changed human environment that our runaway, freewheeling civilization has visited on us. But one cannot force the emergence of a real culture. It begins when imagination catches fire, and objects and actions become life symbols, and the new life symbols become motifs of art. Art, which formulates and fixes human ways of feeling, is always the spearhead of a new culture. For culture is the objective record of developed feeling.

> What really fulfills and establishes a culture, however, is not art, but something that follows—the deeply and tacitly felt life of overt action, institutions, ways of living, things produced. We do not know what the driving force and the substance of the next cultural epoch will be, but I suspect that, as so often in nature, the same development which is breaking the old frame of our thinking will fashion the new one: namely, the development of science.

Perhaps Professor Langer is right. Physics broke the old frame; biology may be fashioning the new. In fact, the characteristic mode of the new age may already govern biology. Its language is not denotative but ideographic—arcane, perhaps, but made up of image bits fashioned together; reality for biology lies not in ultimate elementary particles, as for physics, but in associations which are purpose-oriented. Its systems are narratives of how and why—scenarios of life and death in fully human terms—messenger RNA's that couple with DNA's to be encoded, then separate to replicate the code; viruses that invade cells and capture the reproductive process, multiplying their own kind manyfold; receptors that wait patiently for an amino emitted into the blood stream by a distant organism. Genetics employs not wave equations or quarks, leptons or gluons, but a simple scheme of four base elements, whose sequencing out of a seemingly infinite supply specifies the gene, with the likelihood of occurrence in any one stretch of the genome calculable by elementary probability theory. And if something more general is needed, mathematics is preparing the way with such developments as fractal geometry, wherein a form is characterized by what is missing, its lacunae. These shards of science, however, are flakes from a larger vessel, a well-wrought urn that holds the ashes of an age gone by. Biology, despite its apparent sympathy with more recent approaches, is still concerned with processes, with moving from fact to fact. We shall have to say, then, that not biology or any of the sciences is likely to be the progenitor of the new age, for which meaning will increasingly lie in the completed piece, the art form, not the process.

The central way of the imagination for this new age is *poiesis*, a making of things into culture-forming artifacts. Technology interprets the artifacts and provides the age a supporting economic base. Science, the herald of this new order, must now enter a stage of assimilation (as did philosophy during the past four centuries), relinquishing some of its singleminded focus on ends and recovering its character as an accumulated body of knowledge, in harmony with other liberal disciplines. Education in the specifically human qualities (what we have long called a liberal education) is the only heritage we can give a generation that will have to make the transition and thus for a time bear the world on its shoulders, like Herakles relieving Atlas.

The poetic imagination is the active creative agent of culture, a power that transforms raw materials by raising them to a higher, more knowable state and thereby ennobling them, making of them objects of intellect rather than of brute nature. The poetic way is not goal-oriented, not efficient. Instead, like a dance, like a melody, like lovemaking, every stage along the way requires attention and evokes delight. Poetry gathers, condenses, images, refers, implies, and remembers. By its ability to symbolize something beyond the present scene, it can call into being and make real an entire invisible cosmos. By its capacity for empathy it educates feeling, fantasy, and dream, as well as imagination and intellect. It brings together all the parts of an experience and, placing them in proper sequence, raises the entire configuration to a new order of meaning. To have a rich and vital culture requires the form, the aesthetic control of the poetic imagination. The new society will be governed by the poetic imagination sustained by technology. Just as other high cultures (say fifth-century Greece, thirteenth-century Italy, sixteenth-century England, the nineteenth-century American South) were (lamentably) sustained in one way or another by the enslavement of human beings, a new society will rely on technology to provide the necessary support for leisure. Out of such leisure can develop a truly human culture, cultivating ornament, style, courtesy, and grace.

The culture governed by the coherent "Western" myth has changed markedly in the last score of years and now requires a different myth. America has been busily ingesting its black subculture, altering the dominant manners and morals to accommodate its legally empowered but culturally excluded citizens. These cultural modifications affirm that heritage which black citizens have consciously recovered from Africa as well as the one that developed indigenously over five and more generations on this continent. Having already participated in and affected the American culture, their infusion is more complex and more important than that of any other ethnic group in this country. The culture itself has had to redirect some of its purposes in order to accomplish this assimilative task and, in the process, has broadened its compass considerably.

That broadening has occurred in other ways as well. The fluidity of world populations has brought about an interchange between cultures, western and non-western, that must continue for some time before the scope of the common culture can be determined. Within Europe itself, the Balkanization that followed World War I, with its "self-determination" policy, is slowly dissolving. Both in scope and nature the present culture is undergoing a new founding which, it seems apparent, is governed at least in part by a *myth of equality*. The "Third World" must of necessity be absorbed.

The possibility that the age now under construction is a new "Middle Ages"—an age of stability and wholeness—rather insistently presents itself. Many dynamic processes still current are moving toward a condition of equilibrium, the demand adjusting to supply: uses of energy and materials, innovations in devices, distribution of political power. The impetus will be always toward equalization without the strange nineteenth-century aberration of planned socialism. Equality inherently belongs to "the good" and will tend progressively to realize itself amidst a predominantly virtuous people. When one walks the streets of any small town in America and recognizes that even in the most ordinary of domiciles luxuries are adequate for well-being—that the risks of sickness and old age have been socially distributed and that in fact the difference between the very rich and those a little above the "poverty" line, in terms of the essentials for a satisfactory life, have become very nearly insignificant—then one must admit that a kind of equality has been approached. Wealth has not been redistributed, but satisfaction has. The old motivations —success, competition, conspicuous display—have been greatly reduced. And that simplification is not all bad. It is an unconscious preparation for the new age.

The present awareness of the need for a greater "productivity" in industry in order to compete in the world markets seems to belie the approach of a no-growth society, but in actuality it hurries the situation along. Productivity gains by the replacement of manpower with capital goods and thus frees labor for the production of new devices. But if, as we suppose it shall, an adequacy of devices exists, if what is new simply replaces what is old, then the overall market does not expand. Productivity becomes static. The service sector grows but not productivity. Wealth does not increase—it shifts a bit, exchanges one thing for another, with the activity disguising a fundamental change. Again the situation is not all bad. But it is different, and in it a different set of motivations drives society.

The profit motive, with its bottom-line mentality and its concepts of efficiency, optimization, innovation, and reinvestment, is the happy invention of a rational process based on fact. Profit served well in an exponentially increasing economy. The excess of this economy supported the good and the beautiful—as luxuries, though they were considered drags on the system. Of course this kind of cost/benefit rationality will continue in the new age—in any situation one can do only what one can afford to do—but no longer will profit alone be the dominant decision-maker. Profit will be a necessary but not a sufficient condition and in time will become the *assumed* condition having at best a veto vote in the parliament of action. The ratio, in effect, will be turned over, with a much wider conception of "benefit" prevailing.

An age of equilibrium will have its own set of difficulties, notably in maintaining a fluidity of political structure sufficient for individual freedom. The temptation to use law to constrain natural changes will be difficult to resist. Such legislation, however, could induce large disequilibriums, ever endangering domestic tranquility. Beyond that danger, however, lies the prospect for an ensuing happy society, secure in its world-wide affluence. What will likely be needed is some two centuries of an inverse Renaissance while the present inequities are slowly dissolved away. Unfortunately the reluctance of the world's well-to-do communities and the impatience of its developing segments are already establishing a dangerous instability at many levels of society. Later on, when a potentially violent situation is triggered, it could set off explosive reactions in many areas at once, initiating a general conflagration of great magnitude. Back in 1967, when cities were burning and college campuses were in bondage, it was apparent that the instabilities then present, stemming from deprived minorities and an unhappy labor force, were not such as to be cooperative in destroying society: it seemed clear that civil peace would be reestablished and prosperity resumed. But from the clairvoyance afforded by the disruptions came the uncomfortable premonition that some thirty years from then the social scene would contain imbalances interlocked enough for one misadventure to cause a general catastrophe. That time is now approaching; and though some adjustments have been made and the crisis seems less imminent, still the instabilities are present and the danger has not dissipated.

* * *

For all the importance of Prometheus' gift of techné (the useful arts), it is in another phrase of the passage from Aeschylus' drama that we discover the real import of his beneficence to humanity: "they had eyes but saw not, ears but did not hear." In opening their senses to the world and awakening their imaginations, Prometheus is a true friend to the pitiful human creatures despaired of by Zeus. And this task, the opening of eyes and ears, the bringing of the senses to the governance of intellect (which is the act of the imagination) is the chief function of education. It is what has always been called a "liberal" education, that worthy of free men— the pursuit of knowledge for its own sake, the noblest task in which human beings can engage. The quest for genuine knowledge can be pursued only in that process we call learning.

We need to remember that learning and education are not the same thing. Learning is an internal action of individuals whereby information presented to the senses is transformed by the imagination into knowledge. Information can, of course, be stored directly in the memory by rote and recovered for formulaic use, but such information is not knowledge; it lacks the dimension of understanding. By a kind of rumination, the contents of the memory can be sorted for presentation to the imagination, and learning can then ensue. However it is initiated, learning is an internal process for the individual, pursued certainly for satisfaction and enjoyment, but also to fill a deep human hunger.

Education, in contrast, is a communal process, institutionalized by society for its own benefit: to preserve the ideals and memories it considers valuable, but also to produce competent workers and tranquil citizens for the status quo. A stocking of memory can satisfy, in principle, the educational needs for the *fact* society, with the few geniuses who must repair and advance civilization supplied as "sports" of the process, the new queen bees in the broken hexagons of the hive. Education is an external process sponsored by society for its ongoing welfare.

Admittedly, in practice education gives leeway to learning. Nevertheless, learning seems so simple and elementary, so naïve and impractical, that, in a time of cultural change, it is in danger of being deserted for skills or information. Those in charge of curricula are likely either to design rigid course structures intended to preserve the achievements of the past *verbatim* or to introduce innovations supposedly preparing students for the future. Few administrators in a time of crisis have the courage to design education for the crucial *now* and the perennial future.

For higher education the perennial future is always thirty and more years away, the time when students in its charge will be directing the course of society. It is for that time that education must be designed. In a period of change, quite obviously a curriculum for the new epoch cannot be prepared in close detail. And particularly is it difficult to specify programs when we have little idea of what conditions will prevail when these students take command. Will that future be a time after a holocaust when the world lies in ruins, when engineers as epic heroes must regather shattered resources? Will society have successfully maneuvered through its crisis, with political philosophers carefully crafting structures that will evolve into a happy age of equilibrium? Will it be the time of crisis itself, when spiritual leaders are rallying the remnants in the catacombs to take heart and raise their voices in a new song of praise for existence, seeing in the radiant and devastated landscape the prospect of a New Jerusalem? Whatever conditions are in that perennial future to which the current college age is headed, all will be needed—scientist, philosopher, prophet, poet—not as a federation of specialists but as a unified body of thought, communicating through a common understanding so that coherence is a natural, an inevitable, consequence, and the fragile human race can move to a higher plane of sense and desire.

Actually the crisis is not thirty years away, not ten. The crisis is now, in our present classrooms, where future heroes sit expectantly, awaiting the formation of their souls in order to face whatever difficult tasks lie ahead. Can these young people be the needed heroes, this drug-infested generation, so apparently devoid of morals, impious to their elders, moved by the frenzied beat of a debased music? How we have failed them, are failing them, day by day. We have meant to prepare them, fit them to be the new biologists who will unravel the mysteries of the immune system and thereby save us from impending plague, train them as the new physicists who will solve the energy shortages, instruct them as the thinkers who will form a more efficient economy. We have meant to provide brilliant specialists backed up by competent workers to give substance to our dreams, our ambitions to build a world in our own image. But we have shepherded the young with a brazen staff, with electric prods and synthetic hormones, urging them into pastures not green with the stuff of life.

Of course they have rebelled. When conventions have squeezed vitality out of meaning, then Dionysus comes again, bringing chaos and a hope for joy. The wellsprings of spirit will not be dammed; the waters find their own outlets. The music of this generation moves to a different beat. Imitated and reproduced by countless small groups, of course it is mostly mediocre, but here and there a genius arises. A Buddy Holly out of Lubbock rediscovers that the lyrics of a song —the words—are essentially nonsense, conveying emotive, not philosophic content, in support of the rhythmic sequence that itself carries meaning, expressing some essence of the age. What has developed is a great original music—folk music, perhaps, but a body of ingenious techniques and musical sensibility that will in time find its high forms.

The present generation may well be the best this planet has yet produced. The drug problem will subside, may already be subsiding, but the high profile sketched in by front-page news and two-minute television reports obscures the trend. "Violence in Schools Increases," shouts the headline, but the fine print notes that the number of incidents has decreased. News, one must remember, is always bad news, and the young receive a poor press. But there they sit in the classroom, the best we have yet seen. They have looked without flinching at the shadow of nuclear catastrophe; have survived the multiplicity of things foisted on them by overindulgent parents; have constructed whole imaginations out of the mosaics of an electronic age. They are ready to be educated. They are ready to learn.

CULTURAL MYTHS

1

The New Age:
Unbinding Prometheus

THE DYNAMIC TECHNOLOGISM of the past few centuries, in which one innovation has generated another in brilliant succession, is beginning its inevitable decline. The forces that make for order and structure are rising toward a preeminence that will give them determining roles in society within the foreseeable future. So drastic a change from expansion to stability may not occur without revolution—at the least, a few major shakeups. And it is this watershed in history that should concern us as thinkers and educators. The principal task of higher education in our time is to prepare prudent and dedicated leaders for this crisis.

What we need to recognize from certain signs about us—if I may express it in mythological rather than literal terms—is that the reconciliation between Prometheus and Zeus, an event that the Western mind has long anticipated, is imminent. Prometheus, we recall, rebelled against divine order by giving man the gift of fire—the symbol of divine intelligence—stolen from Hephaestus' forge. Some accounts, in slight variation, interpret Prometheus' gift as instruction in the useful arts (techné), the technological skills by which men build civilization. Aeschylus' *Prometheus Bound* portrays the Titan as author of both gifts, imaginative understanding and ingenious craft, united in the symbol of fire. Near the beginning of the drama, Prometheus speaks of the violence of his act of bringing both consciousness and technology to humanity:

> For giving unto mortal man
> His greatest boon, I am bound hand and foot
> Unto this fate. I stole the gift of fire
> The source of wisdom, teacher of all arts
> To human kind, and for such violence
> Am lifted up to pay the penalty.
>   (tr. C. W. Mendell)

This theft of so mighty a power, even though man did not himself do the deed, allows the human race to declare its independence from divine order and, through imagination and inventiveness, elevate the human lot. Humanity can challenge the gods by constructing a purely secular order that will conserve and further the accomplishments of each generation. Before Prometheus' bold deed, people lived their lives immersed in their culture, unknowing, like fish in water:

> First know ye then
> That men had eyes and saw not, ears they had
> But could not hear. Like figures in a dream
> They lived their long lives out, by merest chance
> All things were done.

Prometheus taught human beings numbers, letters, mining, farming, navigation, cosmological measurements; he showed them how to harness beasts of burden and read portents. "Prometheus taught *all* arts to humankind," as Aeschylus has him assert. History originates with the Titan's theft, just as civilization and perpetual progress begin with it. But the enterprise bears a stain of guilt; for sacrilege and pride, as well as benevolence, played a part in its impulse. Pinioned on the stony cliffs at the world's edge, suffering agony that only an immortal could endure, Prometheus finds again his godhead; he looks into the future and foretells the coming of a deliverer. Zeus will alter his intransigence and at long last seek reconciliation with the Titan:

For he shall rue this day, his towering rage
Shall vanish wholly in humility.
Peace shall he make but peace when he engage
Humbly to seek a pact of love with me.

Prometheus avoids mention of the change that must per-
force come to himself: he, too, will be tempered, in such a
way as to modify his recklessness. Hints of a salvific future
emerge throughout the drama; and from other sources we
know that Aeschylus' lost play *Prometheus Unbound* deals
with the reconciliation between Zeus and Prometheus, or, as
we might say, between order and freedom, intellect and
imagination.

Back before the reign of intellect among the gods, Prometheus, a Titan, joined with Zeus and the other Olympians to
defeat the Titans supporting Chronos in a contest for
supremacy. After the victory, Zeus rules in dread of the
usurper who, it is prophesied, will dethrone him as he sup-
planted his father and his father the father before him,
Uranus. His clear mind holding within itself knowledge of the
right order of things, Zeus nonetheless can fumble in the
making process: the human race he has fashioned is flawed
and should be destroyed. Prometheus, being a Titan, is closer
to the earthy qualities of human beings and, feeling pity for
the poor creatures, steals for them divine fire from Olympus.
This spark of creativity in mortals averts their destruction by
rendering them less despicable. Mankind prospers from the
gift, but Prometheus is hurled into Tartarus as punishment,
with an eagle perpetually devouring his liver. Hence the
useful arts men develop from Prometheus' gift must be exercised without governance by the absent Titan—without
divine guidance, that is, which would enable them to exercise
imagination wisely. History as we know it has been developed
while Prometheus lies bound in his stony place.

Such a myth as the Prometheus myth, erupting from the
thin layer of awareness lying just under consciousness, is, like

all true myths, essentially oracular, requiring interpretation. For myth voices in symbolic figures the psyche of society. Mythological aspiration is the high work of the communal imagination, the "supreme fiction." When the soul shifts its desire, the ages alter their direction. Myth thus mirrors the earthly destiny not of individuals but of humanity, its figures presenting a grammar of human nature and its relation to the universe. Sometimes, from its timeless wisdom, it implies a critique of a present order that the collective social consciousness tries in vain to suppress. If we read a myth attentively, therefore, seeing and accepting the fullness of its images, we can look on the painful alterations of a changing society with greater tolerance and understanding.

The Promethean myth carries with it a fundamental paradox about good and evil that has long characterized the course of progress for humankind. Is Prometheus, pinned in a cruciform position, suffering for mankind, an intuition of the coming of Christ? Or is he Lucifer in rebellion against Supreme Power, seducing man with forbidden knowledge? Is his act in altering the destiny of the human race *hybris* or altruism? Does the language he taught lead to malediction or song? his mathematics to creation or destruction? Various ages have interpreted the myth variously. Further, the effects of Prometheus' aid share in the very ambiguity of his act. Hence his gift, civilization, can be viewed only in a double light: as a curse and blessing. It is not surprising that, at periods of cultural change, when civilization has faced fundamental choices determining its destiny, the Promethean myth has surfaced: specifically, in fifth-century Athens and, two thousand years later, during the Renaissance. It began reappearing, with a new interpretation of the Titan, in the nineteenth and twentieth centuries; and now, at the end of the modern age, it reveals another aspect of its meaning.

What does it mean to unbind Prometheus? It means first of all that in the human mind the two basic divine principles governing the universe will be reconciled: Zeus learns mercy, Prometheus learns moderation. In terms of the myth here employed as the vehicle of analogy, Prometheus represents dynamic progress. Zeus represents order and stability. The most obvious application of this myth to human history, if we are using this schematism, would place Prometheus, unbound, in control for at least the last four hundred years, which have without doubt constituted a time of growth and expansion. In the coming age, which promises to be an epoch of equilibrium, it would seem that Zeus will assume authority.

For present purposes, I choose to read the myth differently. The age we have been living through has indeed been a Promethean age; but Prometheus has been bound to the rock, not free to instruct humanity in the exercise of his gifts. Zeus has been off in his realm, more or less ignoring the human race during this period. According to my predictions, we are entering a time of greater wholeness, when the two principles will be in balance. The unbinding of Prometheus represents the coming together, the reconciliation, of the two: In general, Zeus and the other Olympians have had little to do with ordinary mortals, though they have always been much concerned with heroes, who are half gods. Prometheus, the champion of the common man, has lain pinned to a rock; hence the human creatures have had to struggle along independently, making the best of things with the gifts of imagination and the capacity to invent the technical arts. And we could say that they have done rather well, even—if we may engage in a bit of fantasy—probing the very heavens with their space ships (given such names, significantly, as *Discoverer* and *Challenger*). To go on with it: Zeus feels threatened by these upstarts he could have once obliterated. To destroy them now would require so mighty a bolt that Olympus itself would disintegrate. What can be done? He can call on his old confederate Prometheus; persuade Chiron, the wounded teacher and healer, to take Prometheus' place in Tartarus;

send Herakles, the great hero, out to cut Prometheus loose
and bring him back as friend and advisor. Prometheus will
know how to handle this ambitious race. He has compassion:
he has imagination. He can change these obstreperous
human beings into allies. It is at this point—that is to say,
now—that Zeus will bring Prometheus back to reign in harmony with the plan of Zeus.

The unbinding of Prometheus means that the rigidity of
law and order, personified as Zeus, will become more com-
pliant with humanity, with compassion informing justice. It
means, too, that imagination, represented by Prometheus,
will cast off its chains to range more fully through the works
of the world, as its divine component rejoins the ingenuity of
the human race; and it means finally, metaphysically, that a
great wrong, the punishment for a virtuous act, has been
righted, and the taint of sin removed from knowledge. So
goes the myth according to the revised version that fits our
time.

The problems society will confront in the new age, I am
predicting, will be in many ways different from those of the
past—and not, as one might suppose from an increasing complexity in human affairs. Quite the contrary. It is the simplicity of life that will be difficult to manage. Mankind has lived
for a very long time—perhaps from the beginning of civilization—in a situation of growth. His has been an exponentially
expanding world. The population has doubled and then
redoubled and continues to double. So, too, does knowledge.
In this last stage of the bound-Promethean age (from 1600 to
the present) real wealth has grown even faster, so that, in the
technologized worlds at least, both rich and poor become
continuously richer. The discrepancies between the two
classes may increase; but even the poorest are better off
because everything expands. Mobility has increased from
twenty-five to over twenty-five thousand miles an hour. More
energy is supplied to satisfy our needs in a few years than has

been used in all previous history. We have lived in abundance and no doubt have been prodigal. Certainly we have been affluent, with an opulence that has come from the exponentially increasing expenditures of a growing society.

But that entire pattern is changing. We are leveling off toward a stable population in this country. If I read the signs correctly, by about the turn of the century the population curve will flatten out at just under three hundred million. Not that there is not room for more; doubling the present population would require only about a four-percent increase in arable land. Food is available, pollution is controllable: we could accommodate a much larger population. But the style, the mood, the sense of destiny has changed. Actually, it changed quite a few years back, before the present enthusiasm for population control and ecological constraints were underway. With the change of style a leveling off has been inevitable. And the consequent stability will bring new problems of instability, for which we are manifestly unprepared. For the problems of operating a growing society are as different from those of managing a static population as riding a bicycle is from balancing on one standing still.

During this next decade the world will solve many of the problems which at present appear to bulk exceedingly large. The supply of energy, for example, will not be the barrier which our rapidly increasing need for fossil fuel would seem to indicate. Not only will vast new reserves be discovered under the seas, but nuclear energy will become common as the power industry comes to accept the necessary inefficiency of the fission process and the public to recognize its minimal dangers. This change in attitude will leave for a later time the taming of fusion, which has already defied our technology for twenty-five years. Nonetheless, fusion represents the possibility for vastly greater power which can be realized if the demand for energy continues to increase exponentially. But just as with the slowing down of population growth, a leveling off in energy consumption will become the style. Already a miniaturization of power and of material is evident, with the world moving, culturally and economically, toward information rather than goods as the exchange force that binds its international market together. The communication-handling tools will be well developed—all the optical and electromagnetic devices which will diminish material transport will be well in hand, and the mini-computer will be as common, even in the home, as a telephone. These devices will simplify rather than complicate life and when perfected will become essentially invisible. They will be used but not noticed in the ordinary course of events, serving the operation of society but not dictating its choices.

All these tasks will be accomplished, these problems of techné solved. What I am proposing then is not an increasing tempo of technological innovation, but a decreasing one—a substantially zero growth in new devices. There will be development and improvement all along, of course, but the urge for innovation in material things will be over before the turn of the century. It will be out of style.

In seeking an example for the cessation of innovations, one could point to sports. The great games as we know them were invented in a relatively short period; no new games have since appeared. Our imaginations do not turn to new games. In my idle reflective moments, whenever I decide to invent a new game, putting in all the desirable traits, the game I come up with is football. We could date the beginning of football with the day at Rugby in 1823 when Will Webb Ellis grabbed the pig bladder and ran for a touchdown instead of kicking it as he was supposed to do. Actually 1850 might be a more likely date, when vulcanized rubber with leather cover made the ball practical; or perhaps 1863, when the rules of soccer were formulated and rugby became clearly different; or 1880, when Walter Camp introduced the scrimmage into American football. In any case, all three—soccer, rugby, and football—

came into being during a short span of time. Hockey, as a variant of rugby, was started at McGill University in 1870. Baseball, which like soccer has very ancient forebears, took on its modern form in 1845 with the organizational work of Alexander Jay Cartwright of the New York Knickerbockers. Basketball was a deliberate invention of the Reverend James Naismith at the YMCA in Springfield, Massachusetts, in December, 1891.

All these innovative mutations in sports occurred in something like a forty-year period. Since then, despite many modifications and rule changes, the games remain essentially the same, with increasing popular support and enthusiasm.

Why the decline in innovation? Fundamental changes have stopped because the games are adequate to our desires. We might maintain that a certain level of satisfaction has been reached—a fullness of form, as Aristotle said in describing the development of tragedy. And certainly no epoch since his time has improved on Greek tragedy; it recurred one other time, in England, during the late sixteenth century. But the form attained two thousand years earlier by Aeschylus, Sophocles, and Euripides in a fifty-year span and recognized by Aristotle as complete a few years later is still clearly the summit of achievement in that genre. What I am saying is that by analogy the presently conceivable technological innovations are likely to take the same path of brilliant innovation and then solidification: to bring us to a level of satisfaction that will remove the urge for inventiveness.

Admittedly, one can think of many material things still to be accomplished—the entire biological field is still very much open, with the processes of sight and thought so poorly understood that artificial organs for these functions are impractical. And psychological and sociological conditions seem to be harmed as much as they are helped by any meddling with them in our present state of knowledge. But the innovations these fields call for are those affecting the quality of life, not the economy. They will absorb the small free investable income on which any growth in the Gross National Product depends, and total wealth will become static.

Such a situation poses tremendously difficult political issues —issues having to do with distribution of funds between rich and poor, with freedom of choice and a planned society. These concerns will come to a head just before the turn of the century, when our nation is likely to see some turbulent times. And, because the problems we shall then confront are simple in the sense of being elemental and static, they may be more difficult to solve than those presented by the complex and dynamic society of the past several centuries, where growth alone has proved sufficient solution.

When Prometheus and his arts of civilization are no longer seized from the gods, when this Titanic figure becomes reconciled to "law and order" and settles down to the tasks of extending achieved technological innovations into every corner of life—that is to say, when the task of building culture and not civilization dominates—an extreme danger arises. To cease expanding is to risk disintegration. It was such a situation as this that Rome faced in the fourth and fifth centuries; and her failure to deal with it successfully led to what historians have labelled the dark ages, those centuries when the good of civilization was lost, before medieval culture emerged. A second alternative, no less horrifying in prospect, would be the reign of a Zeus who has not been softened in his tyranny —one who in the name of efficiency and stability oversees a planned society. Something like Dostoevsky's Grand Inquisitor comes to mind. Disintegration or totalitarianism—these are the two extremes that must be avoided if our society is to move into the benefits of an age in which Zeus and Prometheus are reconciled.

If I picture a world static in size, resources, and wealth, a world given over to assimilating its achievements, I do not mean to imply a society lacking in opportunity, unresponsive to imagination and moral leadership. That world will be desperately in need of liberally educated persons. People who understand the past are the very ones who must design the future society, the society of equilibrium, in such a manner that nothing of value in what is now the present will be lost.

It will be those of the present college age who will have to forge new economic and political structures to enhance rather than diminish individual freedoms. Their generation will have to take command at a time when lessening growth and disappearing profits will seemingly invite a planned economy. Theirs will be the responsibility for allowing new institutions to develop and old ones to decay when the constancy of overall wealth brings inevitable conflicts. They will have to choose between deserving contenders when one person's gain is another's loss instead of all gaining together as at present. These future leaders need an understanding of human relationships sound and flexible enough to guide the course of a reconstituted society. Their piety toward their country must make smooth the rough junctures of internationalism. They will have to possess in themselves sufficient magnanimity and courage to take on the roles of leadership required by unfamiliar situations. Those fortunate youngsters now receiving a liberal arts education, by virtue of their disposition and understanding, will be best suited to fashion a new age without loss of the old.

The conditions for revolution will be present in the near future; I should say in the mid-1990's. But if wisdom in leadership is available, the nation can make the transition without violence. The point of my emphasis is that the kind of education we are providing now, the imagination we are fostering, the human wisdom we are instilling, will determine our very survival in the quite near future.

From the beginning of time, imagination has turned toward ingenuity, wisdom toward rationality. The divergence of the two has left a void in the experience of the human race. This incompleteness will be resolved when divinely powered imagination and *diké*, knowledge of justice and law, cooperate in human destiny. Prometheus can learn restraint; Zeus can learn mercy. But in the tales coming down to us, there are two mysterious elements: it is through the suffering hero Herakles and the wounded teacher and healer Chiron that the miracle of reconciliation is accomplished. The heroic spirit and education—these are resources that we shall need in bringing together peaceably the mammoth opposing forces which will create a new epoch in human history.

2

A Spectre of the Past:
Renouncing Faust

THE AMBIGUITY OF SCIENCE as both divine gift and forbidden knowledge resolves itself for the polytheistic Greeks as a contest between two conflicting gods. Prometheus chooses the mantle of man and steals Olympian fire to bring the useful arts to his sponsored underlings. As punishment he suffers seemingly inordinate torment at the command of Zeus. But however impious his deed, the sacred spark proves beneficial and even essential to the human race.

Within Judaic monotheism, no other gods being available, man himself commits the theft, stealing the fruit of knowledge under the malevolent sponsorship of a rebel angel. Exile from a paradisal state is his punishment, though the ultimate outcome offers a possibility of greater good than the original condition. The ambiguity remains unresolved, and in subsequent Christian thought the quest for knowledge that can avoid sin and yet radically improve humanity's lot becomes a confusing imperative for the pitiful human wretches, pulled between good and evil.

The Faust legend, which has become the great modern myth affecting our view of science and technology, grew out of this Biblical legacy. As Harry Levin has commented, Faust "emerged from the flickering limbo between the admonitions of the Middle Ages and the aspirations of the Renaissance."

He goes on to say, "More particularly, he was begotten by the Reformation out of the Teutonic north. . . ." The tale appeared suddenly in sixteenth-century Germany and spread rapidly throughout the continent. An undue emphasis on historical verification in this dawning age of fact led to the conviction that a Dr. Faustus must have existed somewhere at some time. Hence the *Faustbuch* account in 1587 of the "life, deeds, and death of Dr. John Faust, widely known magician and necromancer." By 1592 this story was translated into English, and Christopher Marlowe must have then encountered it. Like other serious playwrights throughout the ages, like Aeschylus in particular, who appropriated the Prometheus mythologem and gave it lasting form, Marlowe sought fables of human action for his dramas, fables that recount in different ways archetypal stories of human destiny. He made of the Faust legend a myth that, inspiring both dread and admiration, would be deeply disturbing to the modern psyche. As its subsequent renditions in poetry, music, and painting testify, for four centuries the Faust figure has provided a chilling exemplum of man's perversion of knowledge. It has taken on the character of popular myth and in our time emerges chiefly in science fiction and melodrama. But its shadow haunts our whole society.

The specific vehicle for expressing this sense of an ancient, ambiguous wrong in which we are all implicated is a plot that focuses on the secret fear and temptation of an entire age as its stands on the brink of an enormous intellectual influx. That fear concerns the lust for knowledge as a means to power. Jacob Bronowski credits Francis Bacon with first using the phrase "knowledge as power" in 1620, twenty-seven years after Marlowe wrote his play. But a poet can be aware of the *topoi* of his age long before these obsessive themes become consciously known by philosophers. And *Dr. Faustus* stands at a highly charged *nexus*, a meeting place of three ages: it draws upon medieval thought in treating the theme of sin and damnation, upon that of the Reformation in the theme of a contract with the devil and a resultant inability to repent, upon an incoming modernity in the theme of misused knowledge. Later, science would come to be identified with that tripartite concern; but in the Renaissance mind, before science had achieved its dominance, an awakening sense of inordinate desire and rebellious purpose gave the Faust legend its prophetic authority.

The movement from the medieval to the modern world view was not gradual; it took place less in a steady growth and development than in a sudden and complete regrouping around a different center, from the divine to the human. In such cultural changes, the balance suddenly shifts, causing a violent rearrangement of old ingredients. Science played its part in this metamorphosis; but science was not its cause. It is more that, within the new world view, scientific faculties found themselves called upon in a new way. If man is to control his world and direct its progress, as he attempted to do in succeeding centuries, he must have power over nature—power to know and to do.

Marlowe's *Dr. Faustus* dramatizes an awareness of the possibilities of knowledge as power: hence it is not at all medieval in spirit. It was composed, as we have indicated, when a new secular attitude toward human purposes and ends was widespread; the play was popular enough to be performed all over Renaissance England. And yet *Dr. Faustus* is within the old tradition in being a morality play, similar in many ways to *Everyman*. Both dramas are about the ultimate destiny of the soul; both show their protagonists summoned to keep a final appointment in which they face judgment; both treat their characters as types; both are didactic, pointing a fairly grim moral. But these two plays, separated by little more than a century, are out of two distinct worlds. Their views of human destiny and the entire universe of thought they represent are strikingly different. *Dr. Faustus* has moved out of a genial and optimistic medieval world view into an epoch that is at once more human-centered and more darkly precarious.

The archetypal concern of *Faustus*, man's attempt to rise beyond his station by means of unwarranted knowledge, goes farther back than the *Faustbuch*, back to the Garden of Eden. It is in one sense a reenactment of the fall of man. Forbidden knowledge, however, is not a theme for *Everyman*, where the protagonist's sin has been a shallow pursuit of pleasure, without thought of his soul. For Everyman, in contrast with Faust, knowledge is on the side of good, marking a turning point and beginning the process of redemption.

Nor is knowledge considered a dangerous thing in the *chef d'oeuvre* of the Middle Ages, the *Divine Comedy*, that great panoramic poem depicting the full sweep of medieval thought and imagination. In it the *Cherubs* (angels characterized by knowledge) stand next to *Seraphs* (those characterized by love), in proximity to the Godhead. Knowledge is so beneficial, in fact, that Dante the pilgrim must continue learning all the way on his journey, attending lectures, so to speak, and even taking examinations in heaven. To be sure, Virgil and others make it clear from time to time that human reason cannot fathom mystery—and Dante is even at one point enjoined to warn people back home against wasting time in idle speculation on the complexities of Predestination. Dante does seem to indicate that some knowledge is prohibited by man's own limitations. But in general vast bodies of thought are explored in the *Commedia*, and learning itself is considered praiseworthy.

Dante, of course, is a thinker, a university man, for whom knowledge is ever to be desired. It is true that he has placed some scholars in Hell, but not for knowing. Rather, their misuse of knowledge is shown to be related to their primary sin. Dante's teacher Brunetto Latini, in the circle of the sodomites, reveals in his conversation with Dante that his adulation of the humanities above all things is unnatural, akin to his perversion. And Ulysses, with his overweening desire to explore, is condemned not directly for his inordinate love of knowledge, but for deception. He is in the eighth circle, the ditch of the evil counsellors. He tells a tale of falsely inciting his men to sail with him beyond boundaries, deserting home and duty for continued exploration and unending adventure. He is probably the closest Dante comes to warning his readers of the damnable potentialities inherent in an inordinate quest for experience and a restless *curiositas*. But it is not a desire for knowledge in itself which has placed Ulysses in hell. And it is something else entirely that has assigned sorcerers, soothsayers, and magicians to the fourth bolgia of the Eighth Circle, their heads twisted round behind their backs. What has so damned them is their attempt to gain unfair advantage by seeing into the future and in particular by using their occult powers for the control of others.

Hence Dante is aware of the various misuses of knowledge: knowledge as vanity and as curiosity, knowledge as manipulation of the physical world, knowledge as power over other human beings. But these aberrations are as grotesque as counterfeiting, as sodomy, as treachery. The main path, the journey for all men to take, is the path of liberal learning, knowing for its own sake, since for Dante knowledge is the child of light. And learning is as natural as loving, both leading on to a supernatural end, in which man is ultimately divinized.

Dante incorporates an appreciable amount of science in the *Commedia*; speculation based on certain passages has it that during the years he does not appear in written records he was likely in Paris studying optics with disciples of Roger Bacon, who had returned to Oxford a short time before. Bacon, the leading scientist of his time, was a Franciscan monk. Late in life he was imprisoned for heresy by his Order, but not for his scientific investigation. His teacher Robert Grosseteste was a physicist, Bishop of Lincoln, and first Chancellor of Oxford

University; during a long and productive life he never encountered reproof. William of Occam, another Franciscan, of "Occam's razor" fame, was called to Avignon to face the pope there on charges of heresy. But his troubles were philosophic, not scientific. Quite generally, scientific investigation was not frowned on during the High Middle Ages.

Science, it is true, had been much associated with the occult in medieval times; but for the most part magical practices were of a benign sort. Alchemy was an elaborate system of correspondences that did not call on the dark powers. Astrology was similar, not so much forecasting the future by means of the stars as finding propitious times for action. Only slowly did these practices disappear after the Church ruled against them. It may be that the outlawing of alchemical and astrological modes of thought (in 1585) gave them an illicit appeal, so that forces of negation could center in them; and witchcraft, which had been long present among the folk as lore and legend, was drawn into the same worship of occult powers. Scientific thinking, in contrast, was not officially considered to participate in magical practices; any suspicion of science centered less on its method and aims than on its specific findings and their possible intellectual deviation from the truth of the believing community.

Some fifty years before *Dr. Faustus*, Copernicus waited until he was on his deathbed to publish his work on the solar system, about thirty years after composition. So long a delay between writing and publishing may have indicated, some scholars think, a cautious attitude on his part toward subjecting himself to censure from the Roman Church or from the Lutherans; but the case for that conclusion is arguable. Copernicus held a degree in astronomy and one in church law, lectured in mathematics, practiced medicine, and acted as Canon of the cathedral at Frauenburg. He is reported to have cast a horoscope at the request of the Emperor, a practice that was later condemned by the Church but that at the time apparently gave him no qualms. He was a churchman; there was nothing impious or rebellious in his thinking. It was almost a century after his *Revolution of the Planets* was written that it was placed on the index, and then only after the whole issue had become controversial, largely through Galileo's constant annoyance of the Inquisition. In general, the bias was toward allowing intellectuals a wide range of inquiry. Nevertheless, by Marlowe's time, scientific knowledge was beginning to be regarded with suspicion. Galileo's troubles with the Catholic Church and Kepler's with Lutheranism occurred more than a score of years after Marlowe's composition, but in those early Reformation days in which *Dr. Faustus* was written tension was most certainly in the air. The whole Galileo affair, to which Copernicus was central, illustrates the ambiguity current during the Renaissance about an unrestricted search for knowledge. Science could be dangerous. Or it could be useful. There was, however, nothing ambiguous about sorcery, soothsaying, and magic: the Church clearly forbade them.

Marlowe's drama is not really about science, much as it has been associated with that discipline. It is about the exchange of eternal good for an illicit gain here and now, a choice that can be made by any person in any walk of life. What Faustus commits himself to is not mere sin, a temporary falling away from the good, but an actual bond with the source of evil itself a contract with the devil. This gentleman's agreement is what makes repentance impossible; a perverted honor prevents Faustus' turning away from his bad bargain. This situation sets up a kind of fatalism; if his good angel counsels contrition and hope, his bad angel persistently reminds him of his pledged word and despair.

The metaphor for the demonic contract is magic. Magic, according to Bronowski, "is the notion that there is a way of having power over nature which simply depends on hitting the right key. . . . if you are esoteric, if you are an initiate there is some way of getting into nature which is not accessible to other people." He sees black magic—erroneously, I think—as prevailing before 1500, giving way after that time to white magic, in which "the magus becomes someone who persuades other human beings that they really are seeing visions, that they really are in a state of ecstasy. . . ." In white magic, as Bronowski describes it, the magus is essentially a hypnotist; in black magic he is a kind of voodoo artist.

Black magic, the sort represented in *Dr. Faustus*, opposes nature, seeks to stop it, turn it back in its tracks, defy its laws. The magician can levitate, fly through the air, transport himself instantly to a distant site. His spirit can be detached from the self, can be divided, can take the form of an animal —a cat, for instance, or a horse real enough to be ridden. Black magic makes use of a power that the magician has not earned. Its efficacy lies in a formalism called forth by a formula, by an incantation, by a mechanistic procedure and a special apparatus. It summons spirits that seemingly cannot refuse to do the bidding of the summoner. The Faustus play quite clearly exhibits all these features: his horse, his cabinet of tools, his recipe for calling spirits, his gestures, his flight to Rome, his unfailing control of Mephistophilis. What magic demands is not that nature be changed but that the magician be granted an exception to natural laws in order to enjoy an advantage over ordinary mortals. Unwarranted dominance is the satisfaction given the magician, his recompense for a forfeited soul.

This negation of what is natural and good, even of the sacred, sets magic in opposition to science and religion alike. Science seeks a rational connection between phenomena; religion seeks an avenue to the divine. Certainly science and its resulting technology questions nature closely, alters an understanding of it, finds advantage in manipulating it, spans rivers, flies through the air, projects phantasms—does in fact behave very much as magic does. But it does so in cooperation with nature, not in opposition. And it pays its way—by thought and by effort. More importantly, science seeks to benefit the whole of mankind, not grant private advantages.

Even though Marlowe had a university education, he caricatures academics mercilessly in Dr. Faustus as he does churchmen. He trounces books and learning in general throughout the play. Satire is a bitter but comic potion. And, with all his tricks and discomfitures, Faustus does seem to be making a contract for comedy with us, his audience. For the most part, the dramatic episodes observe the contract; they are farcical in structure, action, and dialogue. But Dr. Faustus is not comedy. On the contrary, it is very powerful tragedy, and at least part of its tragic thrust lies in the insufficiency Faustus finds in ordinary human knowledge. He has mastered Aristotle's logic (analytics), medicine, law, and divinity, finding them all sadly limited. "Yet thou art still Faustus and a man," he declares in disillusion after his long study. If one would be godlike, one must needs turn to the "metaphysics of magicians and necromantic books," which he savors as "heavenly." The liberal arts have failed his ambitious desires; he would look into a more direct if less sanctioned source of power.

> O what a world of profit and delight,
> Of power, of honor, of omnipotence
> Is promised to the studious artisan!
> All things that move between the quiet poles
> Shall be at my command. Emperors and kings
> Are but obeyed in their several provinces,
> Nor can they raise the wind or rend the clouds
> But his dominion that exceeds in this
> Extends as far as doth the mind of man.
> A sound magician is a demi-god.
> Here try thy brains to get a deity!

What Faustus has desired in his learning is a realm of "power, honor, omnipotence" far beyond that of emperors and kings. Their authority is political and economic; they cannot control the natural elements. The magician, however, has power that "extends as far as doth the mind of man," making the magus a "demi-god." After this meditation, Faustus' Good Angel warns him, "O Faustus, lay that damned book aside!" and his Bad Angel urges him on: "Go forward, Faustus, in that famous art/Wherein all nature's treasury is contained."

Faustus' own motives are clear. They are neither intellectual, nor humanitarian, nor even like those ordinary desires of the rich and famous—hedonistic and ostentatious. His motives are those of a demi-god—to do whatever he will:

> Shall I make spirits fetch me what I please,
> Resolve me of all ambiguities,
> Perform what desperate enterprise I will?
> I'll have them fly to India for gold,
> Ransack the ocean for orient pearl,
> And search all corners of the new-found world
> For pleasant fruits and princely delicates.

He will have his spirits read "strange philosophy," reveal the secrets of kings, wall all Germany with brass, clothe school students in silk, invent "strange engines for the brunt of war." These random tasks, arising from the shifting whims of someone with the devil's favor, ring with a strangely prophetic tone in twentieth-century ears. They are frighteningly like the accomplishments of modern technology.

As he says, Faustus is "ravished" by magic. After he has sacrificed to devils, drawn a circle with Jehovah's name written in it "forward and backward anagrammatized," recited a blasphemous prayer in Latin, he succeeds in attracting the attention of a wise and ironic spirit, Mephistophilis. "Did not my conjuring speeches raise thee?" Faust asks in self-congratulation. Mephistophilis replies sardonically, "That was the cause, but yet *per accidens*":

> For when we hear one rend the name of God,
> Abjure the Scriptures and his Savior Christ
> We fly in hope to get his glorious soul:

Nor will we come unless he use such means
Whereby he is in danger to be damned.
Therefore the shortest cut for conjuring
Is stoutly to abjure the Trinity
And pray devoutly to the prince of hell.

Not witchcraft has summoned this sardonically wise spirit, but pride and vanity.

The magic that Faustus performs is frivolous—boxing the pope's ears, setting forth ripe grapes in January, conjuring a phantasm of Helen ("Was this the face that launched a thousand ships?") None of these tricks would likely in themselves have dropped him into the fiery pit. Prospero does as much in the *Tempest* without so much as a hair singed. Any professor of elementary physics can turn his classroom into a sideshow of magic by using an electrostatic generator and a few curved mirrors with perhaps more damnable effects. It is the very triviality of his desires that underscores Faust's lack of moral judgment. Nonetheless, the symbolic meaning of the Faustus figure gives one pause concerning the relationship of knowledge to power.

In the popular mind, science has gradually taken on the character of the Faustian myth. Such cultural myths, applicable or not, do not easily die. Science remains the inheritor of black magic's arcane powers, speaking an opaque language, employing esoteric symbols. Magic it may not be, but science does draw on strange forces, not available to ordinary mortals. For dramatic purposes Faust may be a magician, but in the modern world he is the symbol of the scientist, the relentless investigator of nature's deepest secrets, disregarding whatever dangers he may unleash. Admirable, some say, and see him as a noble savant, a champion of progress. Goethe interpreted him in such a light and had his Faust snatched up to heaven out of Satan's grasping hands. Others see him as despicable, meddling and profaning the sacred vessels of life, to be held in check by whatever means come to hand. This

phantom is only a shadow, perhaps, but science is nonetheless unable to shake the figure of Faust.

Certainly the figure haunted J. Robert Oppenheimer, the
director of the Los Alamos Project, who on witnessing the
first atom bomb explosion is reported to have said, "We have
known sin." Many brilliant scientists had worked long and
diligently under his direction to bring that moment about.
Does the blame for Hiroshima, then, lie at the door of
science? Might not technology, the use of science, be the real
culprit? The discovery of fission was clearly an event in
theoretical science, and in the ensuing technology leading to
the bomb every step involved new scientific information, so
that no clear point of separation existed between science and
technology. The dominant voice of the past three centuries
might say: If the making of the bomb was wrong, so was the
science behind it, stretching back to the initial discovery, no
matter how accidental it may have been. Even though there
were decision points for use spread along the chain, once fission was discovered, the A-bomb and its more monstrous
daughter, the H-bomb, were inevitable. The very idea of
probability is that what is possible will sometime occur. So
goes the deterministic voice of the Faust spectre.

Granted, the possibility for lethal use is present in any
discovery. Charting the human genome, as is now proposed,
could lead to developments more deadly than the bomb—to
the enslavement of mankind, to the production of highly
specialized beings that fit well into a planned economy.
Should we then forbid such research? For once the double
helix of DNA has been imagined, it would seem, at least to the
Faustian mind, that the charting of the genome is inevitable,
just as was the bomb once Lisa Meitner had revealed her inspiration about fission. Ideas do have consequences: should
we for this reason throttle them in their cradles?

Such slaughter of the innocents is obviously not to be
tolerated. It is simplest to do what we are doing in the late

twentieth century: place the issue in a category of unthinkable, offensive to both moral and practical considerations. But the question of why such a designation should be made might stand a little analysis. In refusing to examine the question of stifling possibly dangerous knowledge, we are dodging a serious political responsibility, an evasion that could in the near future prove lethal. In part we refuse because it is not practical to censor thought, but also because the proposition touches a deep, unspoken conviction of obligation on the part of humanity, having to do with the meaning of time. The shared responsibility of the human race is the task of making time count, of bringing into being the plenitude that life makes possible. In a sense, the fullness of time cannot be experienced without an exploration of the possible worlds an idea projects. It is this existential sense that urges us to make any suppression of new ideas unthinkable.

Time had a beginning and will have an end, two events fairly well established by physicists. Time goes in one direction; for any single observer, time never runs backwards. Events are recorded in the memory according to a sequence of time, not only in the human memory but in things, their present state being, to a degree, a recapitulation of the past. Ideas along with events are shored up in the memory, and though one idea may long lie dormant, when its time has come—that is, when conditions exist in which the idea is pertinent—its exposition along with its consequences are inevitable. The progress of time, it seems, requires it. The suppression of an idea is an attempt to hold time back and thereby diminish knowledge. Irrational numbers, it is reported, were discovered by Pythagoras, who suppressed his findings about them because they ran contrary to Pythagorean concepts; but when mathematical continuity required them, they surfaced again. Ideas must have their freedom, the human race agrees; intellectual investigation cannot be restrained.

The actual promotion of an idea, however, lies in the moral and practical sphere—in the political world, where restraint is a necessary virtue. Prudence demands that the benefits of an investigation be weighed against its cost, then placed with all other possibilities in an order of priorities. Had this been done thirty-five years ago, would the man-on-the-moon project have rated at the top? It had the virtue of being a wholly useless project and therefore in a sense could be considered a liberal study as we define it, except that its motivation was not really knowledge but competition and national pride. Technology may well have advanced because of the project, but who can say what scientific, philosophical, or sociological undertakings were set aside because of it? The super-collider project presently faces a somewhat similar situation, even though it seeks fundamental knowledge. But, sponsoring it now will cut out alternatives, whereas in a few years new super-conducting material could greatly reduce the size, the cost, and operational complications with less destructive impact on other investigations. Practical decisions must always be made from incomplete information and for this reason prove exceedingly complex. Decisions based on virtue would be much simpler; something is ultimately either right or wrong. But in this recent epoch of fact, virtue has been suspect, and if it enters into a question at all comes in the guise of practicality.

The Faust myth is one of the animating images through which the modern psyche interprets its culture, projecting a sinister spectre of forbidden and misused knowledge that clouds our view of science and technology. Yet the Promethean gift of imagination and techné, though it has produced the strange fruits of the bomb, manned space flights, the air-polluting automobile, the urbanized landscape, is nonetheless a blessing. The human mind seeks to know and create; an insatiable search for knowledge, epitomized by science, has accumulated an immense quantity of data about the human animal in his self-constructed habitat and surprisingly has organized that information into meaningful patterns that lead to understanding. What is spread before us is a panoply of possibilities, of possible worlds we might explore. And here the myth begins to assert its subtle fallacies:

The Faust spectre would have us believe that what is made possible by science is made inevitable by technology.

What has been forgotten in the modern epoch is that choice lies at the roots of all things human. All possible worlds need not be explored. To know is not necessarily to do. A gap exists between knowing and using, as between fission and dropping the bomb; to ignore the gap is to accept magic, to endorse inevitability. The Baconian precept that knowledge is power can be seen as not merely elliptical but Faustian: that is, knowledge partakes of the good or evil of its empowered action. But in the gap between lies decision, effectively separating the idea from the deed. True, technology—an action of choice—spans the abyss and is not wholly innocent of its ends. It cocks a trigger; and, though one further choice must be made before disaster results, technology is involved in the decision-making. Chiefly, however, the choices involving technology are made by society at large; and for several centuries a society of competitive individuals, not a corporate community, has sponsored specific technological innovations without regard for the good of the whole. In discarding mythic and poetic modes of knowing, the modern world has promoted a dangerously one-sided growth. Culture all over the world—its forms, its rituals, its arts and crafts—has been unnecessarily damaged by an irresponsible use of modern technology.

The Faust spectre persuades us that science should be reserved for an elite, beyond good and evil, protecting its secret gnosis, occupying a privileged epistemological position, bringing enlightenment to mankind.

In itself, the scientific pursuit of knowledge is truly liberal, free of covert self-seeking, a genuinely generous intellectual inquiry. But it has at times allowed itself to be touted as the only thoroughly objective mode of knowledge; it has accepted privileged positions in the dialogical quest for truth; it has couched its learning in such garb as to be understood only by initiates. Refusing to examine the ethical question of the scientist's freedom to investigate, it has left such questions to the unguided choice of the individual researcher. Yet since a scientist is both representative and beneficiary of his mode of knowledge, the entire tradition of his discipline should guide his choices. The integrity of the discipline is at stake, and therefore the judgment of his peers should serve as guide to the investigator as well as to any funding body supporting the work. A free choice for research entails social and essentially moral commitments. Similarly, the privilege of teaching implies a concern for all students, not simply a selection of disciples. Yet the pedagogic failure of the sciences has been notorious. These disciplines must be reconceived in an overall *poeisis* that makes the quantitative as natural as the qualitative to the ordinary intellect and, further, accepts the validity of other modes of knowing.

Finally, the Faust spectre seduces us into abdication of moral judgment in the face of scientific "facts," into passivity in the determination of ends.

A decision to make use of knowledge is in a large sense a political matter—that is, the practical and moral good of the polis is the determinant. Whether the deciding body be industrial or governmental, it is in the position of representing the public interest. Decisions for exploiting new scientific knowledge are particularly complex; not only cost/benefit enters the argument but ethics, religious principles, tradition, law—all the resources of society may have to be drawn upon, and the outcome may be fraught with danger. But the arduousness of making decisions does not negate the necessity of choice. This situation is not unique to science; any discipline, any human activity, gives rise to the same difficult judgments. All real choices are moral: and the moral life is not easy, either for nations or individuals. Knowledge may complicate choice, but it hardly eliminates it. Faust is a reminder that the desire to use knowledge to gain an illegitimate source of power is an urge perennially present in the human community. Even education, if it is undertaken for the wrong motives, cannot cause Faustus to turn away from the illicit desire for dominance. His is the fantasy of following all paths, reaching all ends, having all power. And yet, as we know in other realms, some paths can be forsworn; indeed, to make a choice is to set aside other alternatives.

* * *

Faust is, ultimately, a phantom objectification of our own fear of knowledge. We have demonized the quest to know, which, though it may be distressingly complicated, is the most challenging and in the end most laudable work we can do. Now that our cultural myth is changing, now that Prometheus will be reconciled with Zeus and free to counsel techné, we should be able to see Faust as a psychic manifestation of an age that is past. It is time, after four centuries of bad conscience about science and technology, to renounce Faust.

3

The Perennial Future:
Learning with Prospero

THE THIRD PARADIGM that governs our understanding of the
connection between knowledge and culture is the myth lying
behind Shakespeare's *Tempest*. The Prospero myth concerns
the proper disposition of science and technology in their relation to education, the process by which society is ceaselessly
remade. Although the *Tempest* stands at the beginning of
modernity, it provides an antidote to that era and, nearly
four hundred years later, a recipe for its replacement. The
modern epoch has depended upon knowledge as power, with
science and technology assigned preeminent authority. But
the succeeding age will require knowledge as wholeness, and
science will have to take its place as an equal among other imaginative paths toward wisdom.

Hardly any question should exist concerning the privileged
position science has occupied in recent centuries. In fact, it
has come to be regarded as a kind of magic. And despite all
protestations to the contrary, scientific experiment has been
rather stubbornly intertwined in the popular imagination
with magical practice—perhaps not without some reason.
Science has an arcane procedure that, as Jacques Barzun has
put it, "once its strange artificiality has been firmly grasped,"
can be employed as infallible method. The scientist can thus
call up powers not his own out of his discipline. This cultic

approach is not designed to be exclusive: anyone can join. But in the esoteric character of science, in the very methodology that gives it power, a filtering action selects out of many the few who can serve as temple priests and rejects the multitude of would-be casual worshippers. For the age of fact, such an anointing of chosen ones has served well as an efficient use of talents; for the coming age, where efficiency will yield to fullness of experience, a more general dissemination of powers will prevail. Science will rejoin the liberal disciplines.

When pursued as power, science does in fact lead to a kind of magic in which a mastery of occult material and a manipulative skill overshadow thought. In seeking domination and control, the scientist can employ knowledge much as the magician does. And, if either of the two kinds of magi expects impressive results, he must give undivided allegiance to the intricacies of his discipline. It was just such singleminded attention to study that led to the loss of Prospero's dukedom and his abandonment to the sea in a leaky craft. Though his original intention was pursuit of knowledge for its own sake (the "liberal arts," as the play reminds us), an immoderate devotion to study induced him into a fascination with white magic and its possibilities for a beneficent use of power. His neglect of duty led to overthrow and exile. Prospero admits to Miranda that he still prizes "above his dukedom" the books he brought with him to the island—his science, his magical art.

When we first encounter Prospero, he is obviously a kind of magus, a "philosopher-king," whose magic makes use of a secret technology requiring expertise and skill; it enchants, casts spells, calls up visions, hypnotizes, stuns, expands time, and abolishes space. In white magic these special effects are instructional devices which the magus employs for the benefit of others. In his role as teacher, Prospero's arcane science opens for his postulants an expeditious avenue to insight.

Such techné has its place in education as preliminary to learning but finally must be cast aside to make way for imagination, the effective administrant of technology. Prospero will find that he must transcend his own knowledge, abjure his "rough magic," drown his book, and come finally to stand unadorned at the end of the play, with his charms "all o'erthrown."

The drama begins *in medias res* at a time of choice, twelve years after Prospero's betrayal and banishment. To Miranda Prospero speaks of the present moment as under the influence of an "auspicious star":

> Know thus far forth
> By accident most strange, bountiful Fortune
> (Now my dear lady) hath mine enemies
> Brought to this shore; and by my prescience
> I find my zenith doth depend upon
> A most auspicious star, whose influence
> If now I court not, but omit, my fortunes
> Will ever after droop.

Prospero's prescience (his knowledge of astrology) has made him aware of the time as *chairos*, the critical moment for decisive action. If his fortune is to "prosper," several strands of his life require completion. He needs to return to Milan and continue his work in the world. But first he must come to terms with his enemies, find and instruct a husband for Miranda; set Ariel at liberty, incorporate Caliban into the general human enterprise; discard his magic. These tasks will demand of Prospero a suspension of intellect and suppleness of will—an empathy—that will allow him to be carried along by imagination beyond the limits of self into a new relation with humankind. Thus the time spent on the island is like Christ's time in the desert or the Buddha's under the Bodhi Tree—the eternal NOW in which the soul's choices are made and the world's destiny decided.

The timeless time on the island is preceded by a tempest, a signal in Shakespeare of the shake-up of reason, nature, and the political sphere (*Lear, Macbeth, Twelfth Night, Pericles*), a turbulence out of which a possibility of new order emerges. The tempest represents a chaos necessary for creativity, a condition in which matter has not yet achieved its form. For reformation to occur, entities must reenter at least the lower levels of turbulence, "where no man [is] his own," and there be made pliant for the shaping that is to come.

A tempest at sea is a particularly pregnant symbol: water is the source of new life, the cleansing and clarifying agent, yet also an alien element that obliterates and destroys. The island upon which all these characters seek refuge from the sea has its own strangeness. Twelve years earlier, Prospero and Miranda found safety at this harbor; Sycorax, the witch, was cast ashore by sailors long before that time, gave birth to Caliban on the island, and before dying imprisoned her servant Ariel in a tree. And now the conspirators who were instrumental in the overthrow of Prospero's regime are washed up on the island and into Prospero's hands in a tempest that, according to Ariel, causes not a hair of their heads to "perish," leaving on their garments "not a blemish,/But fresher than before." It will be an educational experience, an experience of transmutation for all on the island, an event in which processes very like alchemical procedures will distill elixirs from old griefs and injuries, mixing with them forgiveness and love to form new compounds.

The *Tempest* is of course a parable about education. Even on a superficial level it offers useful parallels. One of the principal features of college education, for instance, is the withdrawal *from* society of the recipients, the students, for a short span of years in order to effect a change of stance *toward* society—and indeed toward life. This transformation, as we might call it, is to be brought about by a compressed, symbolic experience under the guidance of wise instructors. The campus as a place of withdrawal becomes a "magic isle," and certainly Shakespeare's *Tempest* offers itself as a ready reference for welcoming remarks to freshmen. Prospero speaks of himself as "schoolmaster" for his daughter Miranda, her "tutor," and there the analogy is generally abandoned as a rhetorical flourish. But a further consideration of the play as parable of learning reveals more telling aspects of education for tutors as well as tutees.

Shakespeare's purpose in the *Tempest* is to please, as Prospero tells the audience in the epilogue. That the author's muse had something more in mind seems indicated by the transformation that every character undergoes before the ship begins its return voyage to Naples. Gonzalo announces the *felix culpa* theme of the play:

> Was Milan thrust from Milan that his issue
> Should become kings of Naples? O, rejoice
> Beyond a common joy and set it down,
> In gold on lasting pillars. In one voyage
> Did Claribel a husband find at Tunis,
> And Ferdinand her brother found a wife
> Where he himself was lost. Prospero his dukedom
> In a poor isle; and all of us ourselves
> When no man was his own.

Even Caliban says, "I'll be wise hereafter, and seek for grace." The play, as we have indicated, is overtly about education, at least on one level, with Prospero the professor and Miranda his chief pupil, the other characters having subordinate seating in Prospero's classroom. But the ineluctable muse is rarely satisfied by so conventional a response. The audience will carry away a conviction that right order has been restored by a series of contrived happenings; but once settled by the fire and in a reflective mood, that audience can begin to put in place the various transformations that occurred and come to see that the crucial change is in the protagonist himself, Prospero. The play hangs on his recognition that "The rarer action is in virtue than in vengeance," and the drama rushes on to its luminous termination. That recognition accomplished, the muse can smile, content, certain that the point has been made: Go thou and do likewise.

The muse at work, however, is not a moralist. Something other than a moral message drives the play, causes its action to come about. The inner motive, as it might be called, of the *Merchant of Venice*, for example, is a dead father's intention of selecting a fit husband for his daughter Portia. The maturation of Basanio, then, is the point of the play, even though the central character of this inner plot is not a dramatically interesting personage. In a parallel situation, Prospero's intention of preparing a proper husband for his daughter, Miranda, is the point of the *Tempest*. Ferdinand is the principal student. If he is not instructed, then indeed Prospero's project fails.

Prospero is preparing not only a husband but a prince, the future King of Naples. The young man is "enrolled" in the course when, after having seen his prize, he is disarmed and led off captive by Prospero. The first lesson is in gaining the docility necessary for learning. Ferdinand's willingness to undergo slavery and hard labor in order to win Miranda is not only a test of his submission and ardor but, as every good exam should be, an instruction as well—in concern for the hardships his future subjects will daily endure. Having passed the laboratory test, he is admitted to candidacy and given oral instruction. He and Miranda are admonished not to break the seals of virginity before the marriage ceremony; in this observance the future rulers are to learn a restraint of passion and a concern for right order necessary to a virtuous leader. There follows then a demonstration lecture with elaborate visual aids which Prospero commands because, as he says, "they expect it of me." It is his gift, his blessing, his hope: that they will prosper and have abundance, will be fruitful and multiply. But the demonstration is abruptly stopped by a discipline problem: his most recalcitrant student, Caliban, has fallen in with evil companions and is about to get into serious difficulties. Prospero must attend to the emergency. When the betrothed couple is next seen, they are "discovered" at the graduation scene, playing at chess. Chess is a traditional symbol for courtship, in which the two participants must learn to play the game, opponents in partnership. Forethought, prudence, anticipation, exultation, consolation, all are exercised in the formal ritual of the game —the bittersweet in victory, the joy in defeat. The ceremony of reconciliation proceeds, the good Gonzalo gives a valediction, and shortly the blessed couple and all others will depart the magic isle well prepared to face the real world, leaving two "racks," two spirits, behind.

These two—Ariel and Caliban—are evidently attached in some manner to this place to which Prospero has come with his infant daughter; and both are shown to represent a kind of knowledge which he lacks. This magic isle is psychologically a region of the soul, cosmologically a place of pure potentiality that has not yet been formed. All the elements of nature exist here in fecund disorder. Despite his surliness to Prospero, Caliban is sensitively attuned to the island and discerns in its aura a kind of poetry. To Stephano and Trinculo he can speak of the strange beauty of its atmosphere:

> Be not afeard; the isle is full of noises,
> Sounds and sweet airs that give delight and hurt not.
> Sometimes a thousand twangling instruments
> Will hum about mine ears; and sometimes voices
> That, if I then had waked after long sleep,
> Will make me sleep again; and then, in dreaming,
> The clouds methought would open and show riches
> Ready to drop upon me, that, when I waked,
> I cried to dream again.

What Caliban is describing is the rich bounteousness he finds on the island, the flow of things, wayward, free, with no higher order to govern it until Prospero's arrival. Caliban is also here giving testimony to the island as a place of imagination, where in dreams he sees images of a spiritual birthright not yet possessed. Ariel's knowledge, in contrast, is of essences, musical and clear, not of things. Ariel and Caliban are thus two separate powers that seem entirely incompatible, as air and fire are to earth and water. One loses freedom as the other gains it—unless man can become the mediator in which both forces meet. They increasingly do meet in Prospero, who as scientist and artist comes to the island to give it form. His white magic is his ability not only to cast a spell and enchant, but to create.

Prospero is a "magus," made so by long study, by the reading of books. The magic that was his inspiration was not the late medieval "black magic" of Marlowe's *Dr. Faustus* (some thirty years before the *Tempest*) but the spiritualized version of "white magic," the beneficent theurgic magic that flourished with the revival of Platonism at the beginning of the Italian Renaissance. The writings of Ficino and particularly of his disciple Pico della Mirandola fostered an interest in science and white magic. Some scholars see in Shakespeare's choice of the name *Miranda* a sly reference to the author of the works Prospero studied, possibly the very volumes the good Gonzalo loaded on the rotting tub in which Prospero and daughter were set adrift.

"What foul play had we that we came from thence," cries Miranda upon first hearing of their banishment from Milan. "Or blessed was't we did?" "Both, both," responds Prospero. And, as he is beginning to see, in every disaster lies a new hope. When one door closes another opens. So it is for every freshman entering college; with home ties cut, new ropes appear to draw the bark to other banks.

In this ceremony of education which the *Tempest* represents, Ferdinand is being educated but Prospero is, all unknown to himself, learning. Learning comes to a person unscheduled, at a time that it chooses, in a place that is nowhere at all. Education proceeds with a certain formality in a particular place at a certain time. For learning to occur in the process of education, the place must be transformed by a kind of white magic into a region of the soul, detached from the course of profane time. In spiritual terms we speak of the classroom as a sacred space, a temple where learning is celebrated. In mythic terms, the classroom is a magic isle, with a magus working his white magic, calling forth phantasms for our instruction.

White magic employs much the same devices as does the older black magic. It differs from the latter in working along with nature rather than contrary to it. It makes use of special apparatus: Prospero's cloak, his rod, and an arcane book. As in black magic, the magus's spirit can be separated from the self, divided, transported, able to be in several places at once. Prospero, it seems, discovers his spirit already on the island when he arrives, already separated into a finer half—Ariel—visible only to the magus, and a baser half—Caliban—visible to all, as was Faustus's horse in the Marlowe play. Shakespeare implies that the two are not simply Prospero's property but aspects of reality. And for dramatic purposes, one must concede a modicum of independent existence for these two manifestations of Prospero: Ariel is freed from servitude at the end of the play, and Caliban not only rebels but attempts to ravish Miranda and to ally himself with two treacherous buffoons—something Prospero's fancy would not have undertaken. Nonetheless, the two are recognizably, in the central metaphor, the magus' spirit. Prospero frequently calls Ariel "my spirit," a term of endearment, of course, but also a designation bearing a suggestion of literalness for those in the audience with ears to hear. Ariel is quick to respond not only to the biddings of the magus but to his imaginings. "Thy thoughts I cleave to," the airy spirit declares at one point. Caliban, the unwillingly obedient servant, enacts Prospero's frustrations more than his desires, yet at the end of the play

Prospero can say, "This thing of darkness I acknowledge mine." Again a surface meaning dominates—"this man is my servant"—but, just as an ambiguity lies hidden in the lines applying to Ariel, so a deeper implication is buried in Prospero's acknowledgment of Caliban. The basic, primitive self that is Caliban, shrouded in the darkness of mystery, is also in Prospero.

Others besides Ferdinand are instructed in the classroom of this island: Gonzalo comes to see the difference between a sentimental and an actual good; the King of Naples discerns the true meaning of fatherhood and hence the significance of governing well; Antonio and Sebastian discover that constant villainy is a bit more uncomfortable than they had imagined; Stephano and Trinculo are led to understand that wicked schemes do not go unpunished. Caliban is the questionable pupil; he has disappointed Prospero over the years in which he has been instructed. Caliban's own view of the situation is somewhat different, however. "When thou cam'st first," he complains,

> Thou strok'st me and made much of me; wouldst give me
> Water with berries in't; and teach me how
> To name the bigger light, and how the less,
> That burn by day and night. And then I loved thee
> And showed thee all the qualities o' th' isle,
> The fresh springs, brine pits, barren place and fertile.
> Cursed be I that did so!

Prospero's entire pedagogical wisdom is cast in doubt by Caliban's unwillingness to learn the structure he would teach, the restraints he would impose. "Thou most lying slave," the magus replies,

> Whom stripes may move, not kindness! I have used thee
> (Filth as thou art) with human care, and lodged thee
> In mine own cell till thou didst seek to violate
> The honor of my child.

And, in a speech sometimes given to Miranda but which obviously belongs to Prospero, he details like Prometheus the
gifts of the useful arts:

> I pitied thee,
> Took pains to make thee speak, taught thee each hour
> One thing or other. When thou didst not, savage,
> Know thine own meaning, but wouldst gabble like
> A thing most brutish, I endowed thy purposes
> With words that made them known. But thy vile race
> Though thou didst learn, had that in't which good natures
> Could not abide to be with. Therefore wast thou
> Deservedly confined into this rock who hadst
> Deserved more than a prison.

Caliban's reply is the classic retort of the savage who has not
chosen to be part of the driving course of civilization though
he is drawn up into it, willy-nilly. "You taught me language,"
he declares, "and my profit on't is/I know how to curse."
Prospero here is a Prometheus who has tried to impart skills
without understanding—without the celestial fire—and has
had to come to the chastened wisdom that Caliban is good
only for the tasks of slaves, to be controlled by fear, not kind-
ness. He considers Caliban "a devil, a born devil, on whose
nature/Nurture can never stick; on whom my pains,/
Humanely taken, all, all lost, quite lost!"

Caliban's case makes dubious not only the efficacy but the
very beneficence of the Promethean gifts. When humanity is
raised above its station, is the outcome finally destructive? If
Caliban is taken to represent the whole of the human race, as
in the Promethean myth, the prospect is indeed bleak. But
everything in the play indicates that Caliban is not mankind,
that he is instead only a portion, and a reluctant one at that,
of the human enterprise. He is the part aligned with the flesh:
impulsive, concupiscent, sensual, credulous, poetic. He is in
fact a figure of matter itself which, as Shakespeare indicates in
Midsummer Night's Dream, has a naïve and childlike yearning

to participate in spiritual joy. (The attempted rape of Miranda needs to be considered in this light—as a variation upon Bottom's union with Titania.) Despite Caliban's unruliness, the cosmic harmony cannot be complete without him; and therefore any educational process must take him into account. Prospero's teaching does, then, as a matter of fact hang in the balance. Small wonder that when he remembers Caliban's new scheme of villainy, he virtually despairs of the good. He breaks off the nuptial masque in midpoint with an apology to Ferdinand for his disturbed state:

> Sir, I am vexed.
> Bear with my weakness; my old brain is troubled.
> Be not disturbed with my infirmity.
> If you be pleased, retire into my cell
> And there repose. A turn or two I'll walk
> To still my beating mind.

What seems in doubt is Prospero's very mission as teacher. To ready Miranda as culture-bearer, Ferdinand as pilgrim and hero, the court company as subjects of justice, Caliban as willing and virtuous servant—these are the educational tasks Prospero has set himself. Ariel is his helper, the muse that makes any teacher effective: creative intuition, or even grace—the Olympian fire stolen from the gods.

But if his magic is not effective, if it does not indeed instill virtue and justice, then the entire procedure has been a deception. Immediately before the apology to Ferdinand, Prospero indicates that he has come to this conclusion. All has been magical illusion:

> These our actors,
> As I foretold you, are all spirits and
> Are melted into air, into thin air;
> And like the baseless fabric of this vision,
> The cloud-capped towers, the gorgeous palaces,
> The solemn temples, the great globe itself,
> Yea, all which it inherit, shall dissolve,
> And, like this insubstantial pageant faded,

> Leave not a rack behind. We are such stuff
> As dreams are made on, and our little life
> Is rounded with a sleep.

This is a sober speech, expressing acute and troubled disillusionment. Particularly must we see it so in remembering that it is followed by the apology, already cited, for his troubled brain, his "beating mind." Prospero faces the failure of his life's work. But he continues to learn. Ariel does not leave him until his task is complete and he has been in a sense reborn.

Ariel is the agent who activates the play but does not participate in it. He is the one character who is not changed, who learns nothing from the activities on the island. Yet he is not merely a catalyst that hurries along a natural process; rather he infuses essences into the turgid stuff on which otherwise no dreams are made. Seemingly he must obey Prospero, but it is in the manner that Mephistophilis must obey Faust—when it is in the interest of a greater power to do so. It is Prospero's desire for good, not for mastery, that controls Ariel. Angels, we are told, have no imaginations of their own, but make their appearances in human imaginations. So it is that what Ariel presents—informs with essences—is phantasms of Prospero's imagination. The orthodoxy of white magic has it that benevolent spirits will inevitably obey what a pure imagination projects. A more familiar orthodoxy holds that grace is abundant and will suffice for the truly humble. To recognize Ariel as the angel of grace is no arbitrary imposition. Grace abounds in the play, is called by name; and Caliban, in fine, sues for its presence. The peripety of the play is instigated by Ariel when Prospero's own virtue falls a little short of efficient good. After visiting the bewitched conspirators and finding them "brimful of sorrow and dismay," Ariel reports to Prospero and adds, "If you now beheld them, your affections/Would become tender." "Dost thou think so, spirit?" Prospero inquires. "Mine would, sir, were I human." Prospero's reply, "And mine shall," sets the action in a new direction, transcending the perfection of the magus for a supremely human, though infused, virtue.

The play is an elaborate analogy, with multiple meanings making use of typologies, myths, archetypes. Prospero is Prometheus, Theseus, Oedipus at Colonus, at times Christ, other times God the Father, the guardian, the soul. But in any of these roles he is the teacher, who desires above all else the ongoing of virtue. And, though Ferdinand's proper education is essential if that other prize pupil, Miranda (on whom Prospero has spent twelve years of instruction), is to have her effect in the world, the most important strain of action in the *Tempest* is the further learning that must occur in Prospero if human history is to continue its advance toward the good. What he is to find is that forgiveness, not simple justice, is the only sufficient resolution for old injuries; that Miranda's beauty and truth must come from her own soul, not merely from instruction; that Ferdinand must be motivated more by his love of Miranda than by any magical spells; that Caliban must be included in the general metamorphosis of the human lot in which Prospero is engaged; that Ariel, the divine fire, is not man's to possess permanently; that Prospero himself must be open to further learning.

What is his magic, what does it accomplish, and why does he renounce it? It is sufficient for casting spells, for making people docile (teachable). It serves to instill a body of information into Miranda's mind, to inspire Ferdinand's imagination about the sacredness and fertility of marriage; to awaken Gonzalo to his intuitive understanding of evil; to promote desperate remorse in the evildoers; to castigate Caliban. But when real learning begins, the magic—as special skill, as technique—must be cast aside. For in the end magic fails to transform. The metamorphosis that Prospero is seeking to promote (to gather up the past, heal it, give it form, and transmit it to the present so that it may be carried on into the future) is accomplished by imagination rather than magic.

And it is imagination that the *Tempest* is ultimately about, not magic, science, or education. And imagination, as the play demonstrates, is that operation which begins with the solid acceptance of human life with its evil and hardship and then moves on to a transformation in which through a refining alchemy nothing is lost even while all is changed. It is in this metamorphosis that poetry reformulates the original terms of existence, "renegotiates the contract," as Frederick Turner has said. Imagination and grace resurrect the dead into a new and more radiant life. Ariel's song is the key to the deepest action of the play.

> Full fathom five thy father lies;
>   Of his bones are coral made;
> Those are pearls that were his eyes;
>   Nothing of him that doth fade
> But doth suffer a sea-change
> Into something rich and strange.

Indeed, images of sea-change occur throughout the play. In context, they signify the *vita nuova*, the new life that, rich and strange, is engendered through learning.

The meta-message that we, the hyper-audience carry away from the *Tempest* is that the events constituting our lives, both accidents and contrivances, can be brought into the imagination and given a shape, an art form. This action of shaping, which carries more meaning, more truth, than facts alone can justify, is a habit of soul as much as it is a competence of language. Its centrality to education was once well understood. That education stands on a basis of poetry is an historical fact, not merely a symbolic displacement. The Greeks were schooled in Homer, the Hebrews in the Psalms. Quite likely the Sumerian young were similarly instructed in *Gilgamesh*. Formally the Greek instruction divided into grammar, gymnastics, and music, the latter being the aesthetic content of all the arts, music and poetry primarily. This poetic basis was continued through the medieval schools, formalized and anatomized as grammar, logic, and rhetoric. Its principles are sound: language must be established and given its aesthetic and a beginning of its analytic sense before the quantitative branches off from it in the quadrivium—arithmetic, astronomy, geometry, and music. The trivium of language is not superseded by the quadrivium of quantity; the movement forward is not a putting away of childish things now that the good manly numbers have arrived. Rather, the quantitative is a fleshing out of language, understood in terms of language. Logic never loses its foothold in the trivium as it fashions operators to work between quantifiers.

Music, though it is nonverbal, is the first act of poetry. Just as logic is the verbal operator in the quantitative arts, so music is the rhythmic, measured quantitative in the verbal arts. In the *Tempest* it represents the work of the muse, poetic intuition, that readies the psyche for learning. Ariel's songs comfort and console Ferdinand, preparing him for the sight of Miranda; they awaken and alert Gonzalo when Antonio and Sebastian plot against the King. Music provides the atmosphere for the banquet, the nuptial pageant, and Prospero's solemn adjuration to the bemused conspirators. Its function in the play is to create an ambience in which learning can occur, one in which the soul is awake and attentive. As Jacques Maritain has commented, the most important function of education is "to awaken the learner's intuitive power"; and it is this role that music plays throughout the drama.

The crucial learning that takes place in the play, however, is, as we have indicated, Prospero's. When, in the epilogue, he asks for the applause of the viewers, he is completing a theory of the imagination:

> Now 'tis true
> I must be here confined by you,
> Or sent to Naples. Let me not,

> Since I have my dukedom got
> And pardoned the deceiver, dwell
> In this bare island by your spell;
> But release me from my bands
> With the help of your good hands.
> Gentle breath of yours my sails
> Must fill, or else my project fails,
> Which was to please.

If imagination is to enter into society and not remain locked in the drama, then we who read or view the *Tempest* and come to know Prospero must accomplish his homecoming. For nearly four hundred years he has remained on this bare island, where the poem ends. The modern epoch has made of works of art small separate worlds that have little to do with actual life or thought. If we are to learn with Prospero, we shall have to complete the act of imagination he has enacted for us.

Prospero is our surrogate in this oracular work that is usually taken to be Shakespeare's last play. What happens to Prospero happens to us. In Milan he is vested with authority, not only the right to rule but the duty to govern. His fancy however, desires position without responsibility. It is his dream of effortless power, in effect, that casts him out of Milan. Yet, if we take Prospero's word for it, he and Miranda come to the island "by providence divine"; hence he might say, with Hamlet, "there's a divinity that shapes our ends." On the island, in an enchanted kingdom, with the aid of his white magic, he can begin his work of changing the human lot. He can prepare a beautiful daughter for the world and manage to draw to her a suitable husband; he can bring to the island his worst enemies, resolve in his imagination all the wrongs done to him and discover in himself the magic elixir of forgiveness; he can recognize and renounce his over-reliance on a skill, on science. And finally he can acknowledge his dark kinship with matter and his dependence on the human community.

This ability to retire into the imagination to seek truth is a *poiesis*, a making of an art form out of disparate and often painful experiences. In an age when judgment will no longer be a simple linear process, Prospero shows us how to turn away from rationalism into a world of creative imagination that will give form to all things human—science, technology, education, culture. He demonstrates for us what life in the new age can be like: a constant process of learning.

EDUCATION

4

The Spirit of Liberal Learning

LEARNING is a natural—a necessary—activity of life. "The end of man is to know," as Jack Burden in *All the King's Men* realizes. And yet, as he tells us, the urge to know is like the compulsion to open the yellow envelope of a telegram—you must open it and at the same time you dread opening it: it has your name on it and, you suspect, your destiny in it. Most of us will open the envelope, must open it, for if we do not, then we become the mediocre, the lukewarm, who, as we have it on good authority, will be spewed out at the day of judgment. We shall not have existed at all. The end of man is to know.

But, as we are all aware, learning is not a simple matter; on the contrary, it is exceedingly complex. Much of our learning in life is independent, a product of the self's interaction with its environment, a synthesis of memory and experience. This learning occurs as a matter of course in families, in work and play. But more of it—far more of it—is a result of deliberate instruction and guidance. Some mentor has to lead and instruct if we are to make our way to a recognition of the high, the noble, the magnanimous. What we are calling liberal learning, then, is very nearly all of this sort: it cannot be undertaken alone: it requires instruction and guidance, communal ritual and dialogue to bring the postulant to the formed consciousness of wisdom, accumulated over history and reincarnated in the present.

For the most part, this wisdom is embodied or recorded in

artifacts—poems, fictions, philosophical tracts, chronicles, essays, works of art, scientific paradigms—so much so that we tend to think of a liberal education as an acquaintance with a seemingly finite set of artifacts. Yet in some disciplines within the compass of the liberal arts—notably the sciences—the artifacts no longer function as generative sources for original thought. Philosophy and literature daily grow with fresh garnerings from Plato and Shakespeare as perspectives shift in their approach. Not so for the writings in science, coming to us from Archimedes or Galileo—not even from Newton or Einstein. These texts cannot be returned to for fresh interpretations or new insights within their disciplines. They are historical documents, active in intellectual history or in theories of culture but not in physics, say, or biology. Such disciplines are *residual,* wherein the active "artifact" is not any single document but a moving body of communal thought synthesized from a succession of works. The works are less important by far than the large construct that has developed over a period of time, to which they have contributed much or little, as the case may be. The other disciplines constituting the bulk of liberal education—literature, philosophy, history, theology, the arts—are *accretional:* in them the artifacts remain active as they gather into the defining body of the discipline.

But even in accretional disciplines artifacts themselves do not constitute the discipline. Some larger form lies behind each work. Certainly, a great book or a masterful work of art, wholly taken in, sheds light upon and transforms existence, but it does so by revealing larger and larger realms of meaning outside the text. And hence it is transformation, not knowledge of the artifact—the printed text or the reproduction—that is the action of learning.

This meta-reality, the objects beyond the books, can perhaps be communicated only in a meta-language; but since such a language is not ostensibly the language of instruction, a more immediate vehicle is needed. *Mimesis* is one that is available; and certainly people learn a great deal by imitation. The first five years of life accomplish a massive amount of learning—an orientation in a human world, a world which we enter, as one writer has said, as though we come into a room in which a spirited conversation is going on, the subject of which we are unaware. The child accomplishes this orientation largely by imitation—by connecting sounds with actions, by responding to actions, by attempting to perform the actions. The child is raised above the purely biological by his growing awareness of a world around him. And he learns all this material by a kind of imitation of which an animal is incapable.

Just a few weeks ago, I had the experience of helping to keep alive a small black kitten whose mother had deserted him (he was about a week old when we found him). He responded to our loving attention, showed an enormous desire to live, learned to manage his bodily processes by himself (quite an accomplishment, it seems), but his learning, it became increasingly obvious, did not consist of imitation: it unfolded from within. It issued in patterns of behavior that one sees in any very young kitten, brought up with an attentive mother and numerous siblings. He thought we were his mother, and, later, his brothers and sisters. And one day, from within himself, he discovered fear. Nothing from the outside frightened him: it was simply that in his normal growth he became more aware of the possibilities within his own psyche —the archetypes, so to say, which we human beings have labelled instincts and dismissed. He arched his back and hissed, not at us but at the great room in which he found himself and at the possibility of evil and violence in the world, to which he would not yield without a show of spirit. He learned greatly, but not from a model. Not by imitation.

People, to be sure, learn by imitation. They may develop skills largely from a kind of mimicry, although to refine techniques requires self-criticism, analysis, trial and error. Can the virtues—both intellectual and moral—be transmitted by imitation? Clearly, young people adopt models that shape their perceptions of themselves and perhaps guide their moral development. Such models may be fictional or historical, or they may be figures out of personal life. If a student takes on a model in his imagination and allows the image to open the potentialities of his own character, he has available to him a totality, a witness to the way in which truths cohere in a living pattern rather than in an abstract structure. At its best, learning by mimesis implies taking an action into the depths of oneself, so that a sympathetic response is established, in the way that a piano string can be made to vibrate in resonance with another. If emulation is an action initiated and given energy by a trusted and respected person, the process can be of enormous value. But if the imitation is kept at a superficial level it is likely to be ultimately worthless and even destructive. When a true mimesis of forms and ideas generates human action, it is not only a valuable but an almost necessary part of learning.

But even so, valuable as it is and perhaps preparatory as it must be, imitation is not an ultimate method of liberal learning. For this essentially metaphoric experience to take place, teaching must strike into the center of a person and engender an action from within. A voice must be heard in the viscera. An inner tutor must be stirred by an external message. The medium of instruction is language—the written or spoken word. And it is the common tongue that the inbuilt tutor understands. However elegant, however satisfying, mathematics might be, it must be translated into the common tongue in order for the self to know it. And the situation is similar for any specialized idiom. The cultivation of language is the real task of education.

What is liberal learning? We might start with Jacques Maritain's statement, "The highest aim of liberal education . . . is to make youth possess the foundations of wisdom." Mortimer Adler notes that "education in the liberal arts is not only an education in the practical or 'artistic' rules of good thinking . . . it is also and mainly an education in knowledge and insight, and in a real grasping of truth and beauty. . . . " Yet the moral virtues, Adler says, cannot be taught. He notes further, "Prudence belongs with the moral virtues. It is formed as they are, not by teaching or by school work, but somehow mysteriously by practice, under guidance, in many ways." Prudence, as he is speaking of it, and as it has been conceived in the Classical-Christian tradition, is no longer a widely understood concept, being largely reduced in modernity to caution or political strategy. As part of practical wisdom, however, prudence is more properly described as a self-effacing judgment of how best to serve the good in a particular situation. And that judgment cannot be taught, so Adler says. The *intellectual* virtues—the arts, understanding, science, and wisdom *are* the subject of instruction. "And here, certainly, wisdom is the highest end and controlling principle in any consideration of means," says Adler. He grants that moral virtues are taught indirectly, particularly in literature, philosophy, and theology. He would not be in disagreement, I believe, with the contention that virtues are taught indirectly in all the liberal disciplines, including the sciences.

More than a hundred years ago, resisting the Victorian pressure toward utilitarianism, Cardinal Newman set it down that the object of formal study ought most certainly to be intellectual and not "useful." Concerning the effect of a liberal education, he wrote, "A habit of mind is formed which lasts through life, of which the attributes are freedom, equitableness, calmness, moderation, and wisdom; or what . . . I have ventured to call a philosophical habit." The qualities of which he speaks are intellectual, not moral, habits. And, one gathers, they ought to permeate all the disciplines—and to become as well social graces. Though Newman does not consider it the chief purpose of a university to produce the gentleman, that admirable figure who "would not willingly inflict pain," he is clearly aware that a liberal education does incidentally shape this paragon of courtesy and good breeding.

In the eyes of any founder or sponsor of a new educational undertaking, its purpose is almost certainly not the production of a gentleman. Some other end is nearly always sought —for a church sponsor, the salvation of souls or the moral education of members of society; for a humanitarian sponsor, the amelioration of social ills; for a state sponsor, tranquillity and affluence. But the ends desired by any sponsor, other than a utilitarian who promotes a strictly technical education, cannot be directly pursued. The most in practicality that can be accomplished by education is the establishment of conditions conducive to the attainment of purposes. Behaviorists recognize this limitation and proceed to systematize a sequence of conditions for leading an inductee to the desired end along as short a path as possible. This kind of conditioning, bypassing any act of imagination, may take place in any curriculum, from classical political studies to teachers' methodology courses. Both efficiency and accountability seem assured by such a procedure. In contrast, the devotee of liberal learning, though he is by no means innocent of desired ends, does not attempt to impose a rigid step-by-step process for achieving them. Fully as purposeful as his fellow educators, he supposes that the actual good of learning, rather than some preconceived attitude, is the experience of learning itself. He trusts in its power to engender a *largesse* in each person according to his own bent. Neither efficiency nor accountability is a primary concern in this matter of enhancing the personhood of the learner.

But what is the fundamental character of liberal learning? Perhaps Newman was too much the English gentleman to allow imagination its full scope in learning; nonetheless he gives us the clearest and most succinct account of the differentiating principle of liberal study. It is, says Newman, the pursuit of knowledge for its own sake, not for any use we can make of it. Knowledge is an end in itself: "that alone is liberal knowledge," he says, "which is independent of sequel, expects no complement, refuses to be *informed* (as it is called) by any end, or absorbed into any art, in order duly to present itself to our contemplation. The most ordinary pursuits have this specific character if they are self-sufficient and complete: the highest lose it when they minister to something beyond them." Newman reminds us that Aristotle distinguished similarly between the useful and the liberal. "Of possessions," Aristotle wrote, "those rather are useful which bear fruit, those liberal which tend to enjoyment. By *fruitful*, I mean which yield revenue; by *enjoyable*, where nothing accrues of consequence beyond the using." Admittedly it seems somewhat paradoxical to expect a useless education to produce a wise person beneficial to society; but it is the sort of paradox that would lose a life to save it. Perhaps more fittingly it is the act of seeking earnestly after knowledge in confidence that all the needed practicalities will be added unto it.

It is an attitude, then, a spirit rather than subject matter that imparts the quality *liberal* to learning. One must come to sense it, to recognize it, and to know it. Once this sensitivity has been awakened and an intellectual *habitus* established, one is not likely to confuse scholarship with learning, entertainment with enjoyment. The human mind no doubt needs amusement—inconsequential and sometimes fantastic fables, bold adventure stories, and contrived concoctions of bloody murder—entertainments of various sorts that exercise shallow emotions without touching the spirit or imprinting the memory. But learning is a different matter. In it, participation, not mechanical response, is required. Something must *happen* within the mind and heart of the recipient. And television or any other programmed device is something less than a happy medium for such epiphanies, though it has been a highly successful—and important—medium for entertainment. As a means of instruction, however, it is too controlled to elicit any deep response of the imagination. For genuine learning to take place, instruction must be incomplete, working by synecdoche, leaving gaps that demand completion, transferring the responsibility for learning to the student. The failure that attends education by visual aids is precisely an over-specification and over-control that terminate an insight outside the imagination and seek to imprint it directly on the viewer.

Indeed, we can safely say that entertainment and instruction are antithetical. Even in the classroom they mix poorly. Some years back, a young doctor friend of mine recounted to me what he remembered as a resoundingly successful bit of pedagogy performed by one of his professors—an accomplished physicist—who affected in his undergraduate teaching rather flamboyant demonstrations. With obvious relish my friend told me of a particular performance: the professor climbed a ladder against one wall of his high lecture hall and, holding against his nose a huge lead ball suspended as a pendulum from the center of the ceiling, released it to swing slowly across to the opposite wall and then back barely to touch his nose. "It was a great demonstration," my friend said. "It certainly must have been," I replied. "What did it demonstrate?" "I don't know," he said, "but I'll never forget it."

In this instance, despite all the dramatic showmanship, learning failed to take place. Image did not couple with idea. Granted, it is possible that some young genius in the room that day was suddenly enlightened about the concept of conservation, to go on to a life of productive speculation. Perhaps, but I suspect not. You and I however learn something from the incident, and that is: beware of showmanship. Entertainment and instruction are immiscible activities.

Enjoyment is the true response to learning, an internal and reflective activity that, touching on a higher harmony outside the soul, resonates in the soul and effects its transformation. Newman speaks of learning as the expansion of the mind and maintains that knowledge is its indispensable condition. "When I speak of knowledge," he says, "I mean something intellectual, something which grasps what it perceives through the senses; something which takes a view of things; which sees more than the senses convey; which reasons upon what it sees and while it sees it; which invests it with an *idea*."

Newman's concept of knowledge is obviously quite different from data or from what we commonly call information. Neither is it pure idea apart from a correlative in the perceptible world. It is something taken into a person, appropriated, acted on, made part of a whole. Newman omits a stage in the total process, an operation in which the imagination submits to the material given it by the senses, shapes it into knowable forms and presents it to the intellect. But he is clear in making the intellect the ultimate agent. For the intellect is the appropriating instrument, the interpreter, shaper, the artisan of the mind that fits and joins the edifice about it. The intellect is an instrument that can be instructed, the pupil of education. "Liberal education," Newman says, "is simply the cultivation of the intellect, as such, and its object is nothing more or less than intellectual excellence."

The term *excellence* is to be taken as signifying a quality—a recognizable quality that raises the intellect to a high plane of action; it is not a mere rank in ordering, a first place in the competition of attributes. Something excellent does not so much surpass other things as it joins a company of excellences above the degrees of comparison, existing in a realm where one is free to consider things as they are. It is like goodness in this respect: the more there is of it the better. Our society rather overplayed "excellence" in the sixties; the editorial pages were peppered with the word. It became a tool of the establishment, a prescription for control, and young people quite rightly rebelled against it. Today the term is rarely used, though the concept itself begins to re-emerge. It seems to be something real, something recognizable, and if we use the term with its Greek overtones as Newman did, free of the false ring of civic piety and undue persuasion, then we regain a trenchant counter for our discussion of education.

Time has its way with categories. The Greek assignment of everything manual to the useful arts and everything mental to the liberal arts quite early shifted the dividing point of knowledge. The reliance of scientific theory upon empirical knowledge somewhat delayed the development of science among the ancients. Archimedes, in late Greek times, was reluctant to pursue his remarkable talent for experiment because of its manual associations. The other "fine arts" too were seldom allowed into the high region of the intellectual virtues. Music has always had an ambiguous role in the categorization of knowledge: though the making of a lyre or cithera was obviously useful, the playing of it was apparently considered liberal. The professionalization of music in the Renaissance, however, moved the discipline back among the practical arts; and present-day conservatories are far from liberal in their aims. Maritain has said that he prefers the terms "subservient" and "free" to "useful" and "fine," since these latter arts are akin to the liberal arts in their manifestation of spiritual wisdom.

Newman assigns to the non-liberal useful camp not only physical but much of mental toil, even that of high order. "Knowledge," he says, "as it tends more and more to be particular, ceases to be knowledge." Specialization, I would add, destroys the liberal quality in learning. It is easy to see that scholarly pursuits tend all too quickly to become illiberal. An increasing specialization, a narrowing of scope, the development of a highly technical language—these are danger signs that a discipline is becoming mean and servile. Scholarship is almost irresistibly pulled toward a reduction of learning to the pursuit of a systematic methodology. Granted, there must be care in both thinking and expression; the most advanced levels of science, philosophy, or literary criticism, for that matter, require some specialized terms for an economy of thought. Specialization is essential, too, in the preparation for professions that grow out of the disciplines. Nevertheless, a discipline cannot afford to lose touch with the whole nor distance its language from the common tongue. A good style in writing is more than a mere aesthetic decoration: it is the very body of the thought, its sensibility and motion. Language carries with it overtones and implications that share the burden of integrity with the denotative message. The liberally educated person has a natural sensitivity for this sort of conveyance. He desires truth to be observed at all its levels down to its very fundament.

So finally I have introduced the word *truth* into this disquisition. For me a regard for truth in all its complexity is the mark of liberal learning. If I differ at all from Newman it is in placing the emphasis here. This is not of course to imply that Newman has less regard for truth, but perhaps that I have a more American and hence perhaps less refined outlook. My primitivism allows me to seek a less polished product of liberal education than Newman's gentleman. For truth, though it be rugged and at times awkward, is still the chief fruit of liberal learning.

The *beau ideal* of the world! In the phrase one can recognize Newman's admiration and also detect his reservations. Newman would found a university in Dublin in order to produce out of these rough Irish Catholics, deprived and dispossessed for generations, a few gentlemen. But he did not delude himself that he was building the Kingdom of God. Rather he was creating a civilization. He would take the risk that a civilization, though a good, might turn to evil. Faith informs him that what is good in itself is somehow finally good. "We attain to heaven," he says, "by using this world well, though it is to pass away; we perfect our nature, not by undoing it, but by adding to it what is more than nature, and directing it toward aims higher than its own."

One cannot of course maintain that a liberal education *per se* is sufficient to create good men. Indeed, such learning may not even be necessary. Augustine, we may remember, in the first flush of his conversion, maintained that an education in the liberal arts was a necessary pre-condition for Christianity; but on reflection he withdrew the claim, having in mind, I suspect, the admonition "except as a little child. . . . " Something essentially innocent inheres in goodness, and education can indeed destroy innocence. For the person whose intellect has been instructed, innocence must be regained by contemplation. In a sense, contemplation is the "action" of liberal education—the ever-renewing, ever-deepening, ever-simplifying movement of spirit that constitutes learning.

I suppose I have meant my point to be this: by our own attitude we can make liberal studies illiberal, can deprive them of their freedom and breadth. We tend to effect this terrible traduction when we use these studies to bolster ready-made notions, preferences, and opinions. For the spirit of liberal education is to be found in the generative matrix of imagination and intellect, the illumination of truth, and the wellsprings of surprise and delight.

We should make no mistake: The spirit of liberal learning is marked by joy. When that joy is absent, it is a sign that we have ourselves blocked the passages to insight and wisdom. We need therefore, rather than making the opulence of the great tradition serve us, to grow to the full stature demanded by its genius and power. For the liberal arts are not merely a received tradition from the world's past but fully as much an ongoing creation toward its end, toward the fulfillment of things. All of us are engaged in that creation. We ourselves are the living manifestation of the truth that "makes us free," the truth that is constantly granted to us in the process of learning.

5

The Three Moments
of Learning

THE BASIC MODE OF THOUGHT of a liberal education, as I am
describing it, is the act of criticism. I mean to use the term in
the sense of literary criticism or art criticism but to imply
something much more general, something that acts on
physics or philosophy or any symbolic form expressing meaning. Criticism is in fact the complete movement of the act of
knowing. It is unlikely, however, that most people see themselves as critics, or even want to. They think of themselves as
performers on the world's stage—doers, builders; and like
most performers they are likely to disdain the critic who
stands aside and comments on the drama of actuality. Yet
there is a part of everyone that does indeed stand aside and
view his own work, his own thought, dispassionately. The
part that distances itself governs one's learning ability,
elevating it to the plane of understanding. The fruit of that
understanding is what one does in life, one's critical comment
on existence.

The critical mind seeks truth, seeks it in a fullness of being
that is a fusion of the subjective and objective. It discerns
relationships and establishes coherences, taking what is immediately before it and finding in the particular an essence
with universal implications. This process is the action of
learning, something I see as occurring in three stages.

The first is the immediate apprehension of a thing; the second is the unfolding and structuring of it in the mind; the third is a truly creative action, transforming the initial thing into something new, which is then given to the shared world of knowledge. The bulk of education is devoted to the middle term, structuring and systematizing, but the first and third terms, apprehending and creating, are far more important to the complete action of learning. These two are so internal, however, that they cannot be taught. They must be generated within the person. One can, I think, recognize these three moments in one's own experience of having fully understood something.

The first moment, as I have said, is the innocent acceptance of, the dwelling with, an experience, its reality taken into the mind as a whole by a kind of grasping. It comes from a love-at-first sight experience, a knowledge of something before rationality sets in, before analysis has torn it apart. Music comes to us in such a fashion and for most persons remains a non-verbal, nonrational experience of satisfaction. The immediacy of music makes it of prime importance in early education, as the Greeks knew, for one must learn early the grasping nature of understanding, that openness to phenomena which is a kind of active receptivity. Music is important also in imparting to the intellect a recognition of ontological unity. What comes to the mind through sight is perceived as meaning, but what comes in through sound is sensed as form. Sight is linear, rapid, precise; sound is encompassing, slow, and suffusive. Poems, accordingly, should be read aloud on first encounter so that the impatient visual perceptors, working with the speed of light and hence angelic in their rapidity, can pace themselves to the more human sequences of spoken language. Poems must be apprehended as wholes before the meaning is evident. The lines "The force that through the green fuse drives the flower/Drives my green age" can be recognized as genuine poetry before the metaphors are identified. But let the emphasis on the preposition *before* as applying to time be modified a bit. Admittedly the apprehension does not always occur on the first reading or hearing—frequently not until analysis has been considerably advanced. Particularly in a discipline such as physics, wholeness forms in the imagination only after long contemplation through analysis; but when apprehension does come, it holds its authority quite apart from analysis. Indeed, if the concept is new, it invariably violates the accepted analysis and requires a new rationale. Physics, it might be noted, never proves anything to be true; it only takes what is recognized to be true and makes it part of a rational structure of knowledge. Truth must be grasped and then understood. The wholeness of an entity—its "beauty," as physicists call it—then becomes the authority against which analysis is measured for correctness and completeness. And it is in this sense that apprehension is the first moment, however late it may occur.

This model in the mind can of course be in error if it is merely the product of ingenuity; but if the image is truly the work of the imagination in a serious and practiced mind it is highly likely to be valid. It emits to the sensitive observer signals of veracity. The shock of recognition, the certainty that accompanies an imagined model, stems from a sense of discovery rather than invention. This experience, subjective but vivid, evidences the success of the moment of apprehension. When I say that this full-bodied, intuitive act of apprehension cannot be taught, I do not mean it occurs wholly apart from teaching. What a professor seeks in a classroom is the moment the lights come on in the faces before him—the "oh" moment, I should name it, rather than the "aha!" moment, as it is usually called—when what was before merely argument becomes reality. It happens one by one among students, not seemingly so much from an adequacy of explanation by the professor as from insight in the student. Over and over, students provide moments of pleasure for a professor by a sudden grasping of a concept which in his inept fashion he is trying to demonstrate. Not his own brilliance but their luminosity brightens his day.

The second, structuring, stage is the arena for theory. This is a kind of mapping, one could say, indicating that there are many different ways to lay out an experience, to chart it so that it may be studied. I borrow the term from conformal transformation techniques in electric fields or fluid flow, but I mean by it something more general. We are familiar with the Mercator projection of the three-dimensional world onto a two-dimensional map, a process that, incidentally, considerably exaggerates Greenland. Mapping requires some distortion; but it imposes a "credible order" upon reality—to borrow T. S. Eliot's phrase—in order "to intuit an order *in* reality." A mapping is a device for presenting experience to the mind in a manner the mind can handle. It is a communication device as well, for we can assume that if the map is simple everyone is seeing the same thing. Any one mapping should be complete: we test for completeness and accuracy against the model we hold in our minds.

In this structuralizing stage the idealization process occurs. A certain exaggeration, or displacement, which is not in conformity with the actual world is necessary for coherence of structure. The heroic, for instance, assumes its characteristic aspects in this stage, when the first apprehension of its image is explored and given structure. Coleridge would call this stage the "secondary imagination"; Bachelard would speak of "deforming the image," wherein a certain element of unreality is necessary.

A theory of literary genre is an ideal mapping, for instance, requiring some notion of a heightened form—tragedy, let us say—not to be found in its entirety in either literary examples or in life, but evoked in the imagination *by* poetry and by certain aspects of life. Other mappings highlight other features— the four meanings of a literary text Dante describes in his letter to Can Grande, for instance. Each discipline has different characteristic mappings, and each of us in ordering experience adopts different ways of charting. The fact that there are many different structurings, all complete, is by no means disturbing. I am not prepared to say that between all complete systems there can be a conformal transformation—that is, that one can be derived from another—but such a relationship is not required for validity. Each structuring that is consistent and complete, representing a serious attempt to chart experience, brings out salient features of the real subject under study.

Systematic thought abounds in the structuring stage. Frequently systems are so rich, so beautiful that they satisfy the hunger for the real thing, substituting idea for reality. "Euclid alone has looked on beauty bare," Edna Millay noted. And, truth to tell, this very sparseness of geometry can be strangely satisfying, in its disdain of the finite. Physics often suffers from an over-elegance in mapping. So, too, does philosophy. Logic often checks against itself for consistency rather than against an extra-mental reality. For that reason logic is not a satisfactory introductory course, presenting a very real possibility that the student may become so entranced by the map that he never notices the actual terrain. Logic should come later, in the position of critique.

Learning in this sense of absorbing and understanding a whole system, a structure, is highly satisfying. For the student, its mastery is a genuine accomplishment, lifting him above his peers. But the process is not complete in the full sense of learning. Learning must cause a metamorphosis of the person, not merely elevate him—must make him into something different from what he was before. The evidence for this change comes in the third moment, the moment of *making*. Something new must issue from the learner, something he has not been taught, that has about it a recognizability of authenticity. Let me illustrate this process by recalling the figure of sound and light I used some minutes ago to demonstrate the primacy of non-verbal meaning. If we take the idea seriously, we give it an immediate validity—that is, we grasp it. Then our minds immediately start rearranging things so that the new concept fits in—that is, we undertake a structuring process. My mind worked in this manner a moment ago as I took hold of the idea of the velocity of light as a million times faster than sound, so that one receptor is flooded and the other ordered. I envisioned the little area in the brain where visual images are given a quick processing before being forwarded to the more interior central unit, whereas sound comes into the larger Broca's area and is apparently more fully processed. Then out of this sort of quick mapping issued a metaphor, that of impatient angels. Anyone else's structuring would be quite different, characteristic of an individual's discipline and experience, and what each makes of it is his own. But we all apprehend the same thing.

For the third, creative, moment to occur, the first moment must have taken place. However intricate and extended an analysis one may make, if the moment of recognition does not come, one cannot make a significant addition to a field of study. The thinker must have apprehended the object whole in his imagination in order to say or do anything important about it. In contrast, the second moment, the analysis, is not an absolute necessity. A work of art can be made out of direct apprehension, although such a work is likely to seem primitive or accidental. All three moments must occur for the process to be complete, for an increase in the world's body to come about.

For a demonstration of the process, I shall turn to one of the great poems about imagination in our language, Gerard Manley Hopkins' "The Windhover," which both describes the process and initiates it in the reader. The poem is so familiar to many of us that the immediate shock of it has long since passed. But imagine, if we can, that we are hearing it for the first time. We know immediately that we are in the presence of a poem of some consequence. We cannot understand it entirely with our rational faculties, but we apprehend its psychic action. It should be read aloud, as all poems should (at least on first encounter); for, as we have said, form is apprehended at the pace of the spoken word.

The Windhover
To Christ Our Lord

I caught this morning morning's minion, king-
  dom of daylight's dauphin, dapple-dawn-drawn Falcon, in his riding
Of the rolling level underneath him steady air, and striding
High there, how he rung upon the rein of a wimpling wing
In his ecstasy! then off, off forth on swing,
  As a skate's heel sweeps smooth on a bow-bend: the hurl and gliding
Rebuffed the big wind. My heart in hiding
Stirred for a bird,—the achieve of, the mastery of the thing!

Brute beauty and valour and act, oh, air, pride, plume, here
  Buckle! AND the fire that breaks from thee then, a billion
Times told lovelier, more dangerous, O my chevalier!

  No wonder of it: sheér plód makes plough down sillion
Shine, and blue-bleak embers, ah my dear,
  Fall, gall themselves, and gash gold-vermillion.

The poem is about the act of knowing, that strange interpenetration that takes place between self and world. The vehicle for exploring the full scope of the act in all its stages is a quick glimpse of a falcon in its course across the morning sky. This is the moment of grasping, of complete openness and receptivity. The experience is so massive and full that the observer must attempt to understand it. What is there to this natural beauty and grace? the speaker wonders, mapping all the qualities of the experience; and under the weight of the "brute beauty" the analysis "buckles," so that an insight (fire) bursts forth. This is the high point of the poem: the beauty that flames out is "a billion times told lovelier" and, strangely, "more dangerous." We must surmise that its flash cuts into the soul, piercing regions that are at the very center of being.

This is the realm of ecstasy, of insight—a region protected because highly vulnerable ("dangerous"), where only the highest knowledge can be admitted. Then after the fire of insight, in the making stage, the viewer finds two analogies that provide the answer to his question. "Inscape," the inner being of something, is the source of beauty, first, for the earth as it is cut by a plow and, second, for logs that seem to be reduced to ashes but that, breaking, reveal an interior radiance. In the same manner, the inner qualities of the bird's flight, when gazed at with the eyes of the imagination, reveal themselves "a billion times told lovelier" than the externals. For the Jesuit poet they speak of Christ's abiding presence in the world.

Our act of criticism, applied to the poem, reveals that the poem itself is an act of criticism applied to Christ's glory in the world—the grasping of divine splendor at the actual sight of the swooping falcon, the mapping of the experience with a listing of the qualities of the bird's flight, the making of a mimesis of the encounter with imagined images of earth and fire. The critical act, then, in its extension over the three moments, duplicates the action of the poem and invites the same action in the reader. In interpreting the poem, the critic must first grasp its wholeness, then analyze its structure, and finally contemplate its totality, its form. And, by a careful attention to the movement of the poem, the critic unfolds in the three stages a movement toward universality and insight. What is discovered is that the poet, in submitting to the rhythm of perception, analysis, and contemplation, has encountered the revelation—in a critical act—of something about the Creator of the universe and His way of working.

"All life is action," Aristotle wrote; and its end is a mode of action." He divides the stages of life's action into *praxis*, *poiesis*, and *theoria*, doing, making, and contemplating. It would take a bit of ingenuity to demonstrate that these correspond fairly well with my grasping, mapping, and making.

What seems more important is to take note of the fact that for Aristotle action is the heart not only of the arts but of life itself. The rhythm that flows through all things, he saw, moves through the act of knowing. His declaration that the purpose of life is a mode of action bears some examination. That action, he makes clear in other statements, is *theoria*, contemplation. To know is the highest good; and knowing is both submissive to reality and vitally active.

For an education to be liberal it must of necessity focus on the very movement of existence; and I suggest that it needs to structured around the three moments of thought. What is ordinarily omitted in our schooling is the first stage, grasping— the taking in, the experiencing—on which the entire structure is built. We tend in our study to move too quickly into rationality. Somehow, for the liberal habit of mind, logic and persuasion are inadequate instruments for conviction. Intuition must be instructed, transformed, if we may say so, by a deeply habitual movement of grasping, mapping, and making, all three stages flowing in one overwhelming and satisfying critical act.

These three moments of learning define the human person. This mysterious creature, made in the image of a seer, perceives the world and finds it good, takes it into himself not voraciously but in unison with it, allows it to dwell as images in his mind until he comes to know it in its aspect of rationality. Then, because he is also made in the image of a creator, he must make something of himself and of what has been given to him. It is this mystery of receiving and returning that constitutes the complete act of understanding.

6

Universal Liberal Education

My INTENTION here is not to promote the liberal arts as the classical tradition, nor to redefine them in terms appropriate for the day; neither to demonstrate their utility, nor, by freeing them from utilitarian constraints, to make them ends in themselves. For, truth to tell, the liberal arts are no more ends than they are idols or instruments. They are merely means toward a goal which has never been and perhaps never can be overtly stated, something that lies just over the hill, just out of sight, just out of reach of our hearing. But if we cannot express their purpose we can at least describe their effect. And that is, as we might simplistically state it, to enable a person to achieve the true form of his life.

From the moment of birth, life is a process of learning. It is the chief obligation of all living things, their chief task and chief joy. Surely it is only an over-seriousness of entomologists that denies us an account of young ants at play, like young tigers exuberant in their learning of survival traits. All things rejoice in learning, dolphins and dogs bodily smiling at the task. When the mind is either satiated or anorexic and cannot learn, despair sets in. "Give us this day our daily hunger," says Gaston Bachelard, an avid reader of books. For whatever reason we learn, from desire, from compulsion, from pride, from greed, for use, for pay, what we gain is joy. "We learn of the death of friends with a sly pleasure/A sense of cleansing and hope that comes from distress," Robert Penn

Warren wrote in "Original Sin," a dark vignette of our fallen state that embarrasses us all.

Knowledge is the residue of learning. The emotional content it calls forth ranges from grief to ecstasy, a panoply of responses to the information and to the form of what it contains. To learn is to live, to know is to suffer; to suffer the little children to come into the presence of consciousness, with all the motley guests of time that enter through the gate of learning.

There is a soul that is the learner, a *cogito* that is the knower, a self that wills to act empowered by knowledge. It is an external world of reality that is acted upon, a world peopled by other selves that similarly act and therefore interact to form a tribe, a folk, a community, a city. My general concern in previous talks has been with this corporate life in which people share. My usual efforts have been to find the purpose of a liberal education in its communal elevation, when it is working toward a well-being wherein all these interacting selves find mutual satisfaction. In the present rumination I want, in some contrast, to concentrate on that simple self that learns and knows the presence of reality.

"Issues from the hand of God the simple soul," T. S. Eliot writes in his "Animula," quoting a line from Dante. Eliot proceeds to lay out for us the world of primary sensations of hot, cold, damp, and dry into which an infant emerges, eager to be reassured, finding pleasure in bright colors and fragrances, in sunshine, water, and vegetation. But, he continues, "The heavy burden of the growing soul/Perplexes and offends. . . . " The child grows, dreams, begins to suffer pain, satisfies his curiosity by gathering information. And then finally the process of growing up is complete: "Issues from the hand of time the simple soul/Irresolute and selfish, misshapen, lame." The poet concludes his paean of pain with a petition for prayer not at the hour of our death but of our birth.

Eliot has given us an incisive portrayal of the downward path to wisdom, in which knowledge apparently leads to sin and diminution. But there are other simple souls who exit this valley trailing more glory than adorned them with Wordsworthian mists when they entered. These are they "who have come out of great tribulation" and have learned from it, the same tribulation from which others come irresolute and selfish, misshapen and lame. But let me set aside these liturgical overtones, both Eliot's and mine, and in more common language investigate what there is about learning that ennobles some and diminishes others.

The instructors for life are manifold. Once out of the common womb, an infant is taught by every object, every being, every event that surrounds it. The instructors vary widely in their quality from home to home, and one must be neither so socially insensitive as to suppose environmental variation to be of little difference nor so genetically innocent as to ignore prenatally determined capabilities.

As for the first, society must do what it can to alleviate and compensate for differences in background, keeping in mind that they are statistical and not individual determinants. The second differentiator, innate abilities, has so small a range on any cosmic scale as to make a concern for it of only second order. The very act of speaking demonstrates so vast a learning ability in even the most obtuse as to make the difference from the gifted almost imperceptible, if viewed indifferently from afar. (The earth is a smooth sphere to the eye of the moon.) The basic core of learning is common to all. Education exaggerates difference.

In speaking of difference, we have obviously wandered into the problem of schooling, as is perhaps inevitable in a discussion of education. And the first thing to emphasize in any consideration of schools is one of the Paideia Project tenets, that throughout required elementary and secondary education there should be one track only for the curriculum. A multi-track system, with children grouped according to their assumed ability to learn, establishes a class structure defined in childhood, a slaughter of the innocents, so to speak. In the same manner, too, a vocational track in secondary schools reinforces cultural differences. It seems to the privileged members of society a kind and concerned expedient to provide a ready path for sustenance and a "way up" to lesser abilities and limited ambitions; but such an attitude is an unwarranted condescension and an unrecognized intention of preserving the status quo. In reality vocationalism is a preparation for obsolescence, a harbinger of frustration. The public is ill-served, both economically and culturally, by such a separation of young minds into workers and thinkers, and democracy is thereby rendered a virtual impossibility.

This kind of argument is important but is probably peripheral to the interest of learning. Education itself is the chief beneficiary of a normal mixture of minds. The concept of magnet schools for special interests or for "talented and gifted" students is a ruse perpetrated by fond parents and bowed to by school administrators embarrassed by the quality of their enterprise. Granted, the problem they face is vexing: how can a single scheme serve both the best of students and the worst? The curriculum is the center of the solution; it must be the same for all students, but designed for the best—not in its complexity but in its imaginative scope and profundity. Ordinary and even lower than ordinary students respond to good material; they may remain less adroit than their brilliant classmates, but they live on the same plane of understanding. And the superior learners acquire from a mixed community responsibility and respect for their fellows.

Let me say in passing that the degree of difficulty or of profundity, whichever one prefers, can be considerably advanced over that prevailing in high school today. The Paideia plan proposes that the level be about that of courses currently taught in the first two years of a good liberal arts college.

Advanced Placement programs hardly seem the models for this improvement of curriculum. Nor are elementary courses in college. Nothing short of a complete rethinking of our entire educational scheme will suffice—a reconsideration of the problems raised by the seeming paradox of requiring both excellence and equality in a curriculum. It is evident that the beginning point for any solution to these problems lies in a liberal education for all.

And that conclusion takes us back to the simple self, the poor little tyke now ready for school. Buffeted about by all the stimuli its five senses can handle, its imagination overcontrolled and thwarted by the realistic fantasies of television and Disneylands, it marches through the gateway to society, the public school. Here it will be fashioned, shaped, deformed, behaviorized into being the unit of society.

Let me not dispraise the public school. Universal education is a remarkable accomplishment. It has managed to offer twelve years of schooling for all young people, although we must admit that only recently has such an accomplishment been made possible for everyone. This inclusion is a great moral achievement; but like most moral gains in the modern world, it came about when the situation for it became practical. Slavery was finally eliminated when it was no longer economically advantageous and so, similarly, was child-labor. The entire institution of slavery could be abolished; but in a society that has thought primarily of the balance sheet, childhood has remained a permanent drain upon the economy. Something has had to be done with the young, once factories and farms were mechanized. Society inaugurated schools, primarily to handle the problem of the child, and took the first step toward universal education. Schools developed in the eighteenth century in an industrial pattern, deserting the monastic and cathedral school tradition designed for postulants. As in other modes of industrial work, in the schools a work day was established, with laborers turning out a product in a batch process, organized around clock-time. And the system served fairly well. Social structures were advanced if not elevated by the stratagem. But now that industrialization is approaching its own asymptotic limit, and the economic world is undergoing radical changes not yet fully envisioned, it is time to reconsider the pattern of schooling.

Most of the remedial schemes that have recently been suggested for public education are not far-reaching enough. Though mere reform of the system could alleviate many of our schools' ills, it can hardly provide the fertile ground for new growth. What is required is a radical restatement of the purposes of education, something beyond a selection of content, something that can guide individual schools in pursuit of their educational mission. How do we answer the question of what should be taught? When asked recently to suggest what science should be included in the early grades, I replied "None." Something much more basic needs to be undertaken before we turn to disciplines and specific content. First the injured imagination of that little child I deserted a few paragraphs back needs to be repaired. The child must discover that he possesses a storehouse of images of real things that can be recalled from memory into the active mind, freed of the tags and abstractions by which an efficient environment has shorn experience of its meaning. The image exists whole in the mind; it has an amazing ability to complete itself according to a loosely structured intuition that very early begins to form in a periodicity of satisfactions. This process can be encouraged in the classroom in the guise of games, an entire class putting together a construction of a familiar sight or event. In such a manner the child learns something about the communal nature of knowledge, about the relationship of the lonely interior of the mind to the busy and populous exterior, the subjective conjoining the objective. This action of the imagination is essential to understanding, for science as for poetry. Indeed, it is the starting point for all liberal knowledge, that kind of knowledge that, free and active in the person, encompasses an objective reality.

And now I think we can safely leave the child, gleeful in its new discoveries, while we explore the ills of present-day education and seek to find a principle of unity for the sort of learning that can lead this little "wise philosopher," this "seer blest" into a fully satisfactory maturity.

* * *

Hardly anyone would be willing to admit that education is not a matter of intellect but of imagination. Liberal education makes use of imagination from the very beginning and in so doing stocks it with images and constructs a communications network allowing various items to become interconnected or superimposed. Creativity lies largely in this process; so does ordinary learning, at least in the sense that learning is understanding. The verbal subjects, history and literature in particular, rather naturally exercise the student's imaginative faculty; but written composition tends to stifle it by an early reliance on rules. Rote learning avoids imagination and takes its material directly to memory, tagging it there by something like a mnemonic device for ready recall. A certain amount of rote learning is demanded by utility—the multiplication tables, for example—but to fill the memory with information can easily stultify the imagination.

In the early grades, children acquire information with such ease and delight that imagination tends to be neglected, with disastrous results in later schooling. The process of logical thinking, like composition, can be end-stopped by formulae and prevented from expanding naturally to fit new material when memorized examples no longer apply. In the prevailing atmosphere of our schools, the quantitative subjects encounter even greater handicaps. Arithmetic is usually taught as a set of unbending rules, not an ingenious invention of the mind. Imagination could be employed in arithmetic, algebra, and certainly in geometry; but efficiency usually suggests a more limited kind of learning, based on relentless drill in rules and examples. The situation has recently been worsened by the apparent decrease in arithmetical rote-learning ability and a consequent drop in quantitative scores, perhaps attributable to the use of the hand-held calculator. Such a diminution is not inevitable, however. The calculator should on the contrary allow freedom for increasing imaginative skill.

Something of a crisis has presently developed in science and engineering in this country because of the widespread failure of students to learn the calculus in high school or college. Calculus is the gateway to higher mathematical and scientific learning; hence its neglect can lead to the intellectual deterioration of our nation. Even though a self-selection limits enrollment in beginning calculus courses to about one in ten young persons who elect to take the course, only about half of this already select group achieve a grade high enough to warrant advanced work. Undoubtedly the failure rate is due to the rote learning of mathematics throughout lower schooling.

Calculus requires a small leap of the imagination in such concepts as limits and infinitesimals for differentials, as well as arbitrary constants for integrals. The concepts are simple, but the sudden shift in basis from memory to imaginative reasoning in quantitative matters seemingly produces a stasis of mind in ninety-five percent of the school population. Calculus may seem too specialized a skill for its absence in a great proportion of society to instill major worries about the state of the nation. But the lack of the *ability* to learn it more than the skill itself indicates a very serious division for a democratic citizenry, with a resulting over-reliance on specialists. A successful technology permits individuals to live productive lives with minimal skills, but it does not lead them to happy lives if they cannot in principle communicate quite generally with each other.

The society that would result from a universal liberal education would find its bonds as much in the arts as in the economy, as much in conversation as in politics. A widely shared active imagination would permit ready understanding and sympathetic hearing of multiple points of view. Liberal education, it should be seen, is the proper responsibility of society and is to be pursued for its benefit.

But it is the individual that makes up society, and it is the individual that must be educated. Hence some view of the human person is necessary to any plan for an adequate education. What is this little urchin, curled up in the window seat? What is this being that schooling is expected to shape into a full realization of its potential? Any answer that we posit to this question must be conceived *mythopoetically*, rather than logically, for any knowledge we have of the whole of the human person has come to us through images, symbols, and analogies. From these intuited glimpses along with religious revelation, the human community works its *poiesis* in constructing the large and intricate forms by which society and the individual take on meaning. It is in the context of these forms that any one being participates in the panoply of relationships that make him a person.

Essentially, one might say, the human person is a soul—a soul from which emanates and which then governs a veritable cosmos, an individual microcosm homogeneous with the larger orders of which it is both a part and an image. At the base of the human cosmos is the dark grounding of the primordial, where dwell those monstrous and ambiguous figures of instinct and apprehension common to all humankind. Images of these forms can thrust unbidden into the field of consciousness with reminders of the contingencies of existence and the certainties of mortality. Above this domain, at the crest of the cosmos, is the region of light from which intelligibility infuses the experienced world.

These two extremes, the realms of dark and of light, both shrouded in mystery, are the givens, the same for all creatures, though differently apprehended. In between is the arena of responsibility, of accountability, wherein the soul makes its construction, in accord with what it inherits of myth, tradition, and culture. This stratum of the individual cosmos interacts with similar strata in others of the community, their federation forming a communal history. What Faulkner calls "the long human recording" is this federated undertaking of the human race. In it metaphysical, moral, and aesthetic values are incarnated, tested, remembered, and constantly reformulated. Within the individual cosmos great constructs are made that span the whole region, some borrowed, some invented, but all owned and operated by the single mind in charge of this cosmos. The person comes to terms with existence by means of these mental structures. The heroic, tragic, comic, and lyric modes, for example, are interpretations of experience with the individual soul at their centers, made in awareness of the boundary situation in which mortals dwell.

Some equivalent of this cosmology should lie behind any educational endeavor, giving purpose and order to learning. Such structures are not, certainly, the content of what is taught; nor do they constitute a system of educational theory. Rather, they form a myth of human nature and destiny, an invisible web of meaning within which learning takes on significance. And it is precisely this poetic structure that educational systems have deliberately excluded. Yet human beings can be fully human only when their souls are formed by the high aims and ideals of their myth; they can know their own capabilities only when they see themselves in the light of the heroic achievement of their traditions. Schools, we must remember, are aids, not dictators, of this endeavor. Individual differences will take care of themselves; what we are called now to consider is the great matrix of meaning in which each of us participates in attaining the full dimensions of human feeling and thought. If civilization is to survive, we can no longer avoid the need for nurturing all our young: in our time, nothing less than a universal liberal education will suffice.

7

Imagination, Redundancy, and the Act of Learning

ANYTIME WE ATTEMPT to examine the workings of the imagination, we need to begin with another quick look at Coleridge's differentiation between fancy and imagination, which is as relevant today as in 1817. Though the terms have been discussed *ad nauseam*, they have been treated as literary *curiosa* rather than as concepts pointing to a crucial distinction determining our perception of the world. Fancy, whatever our word for it, uses the material stored in the memory very much as it was taken in, rearranged and counterposed with little volition. Dreams, in this sense, are products of fancy, but dream interpretations are works of the imagination. Further—and this part is surprising—the *appearance* of things wherever appearance subjugates or petrifies the will is in itself fancy.

Shakespeare was preoccupied with this distinction. In the *Merchant of Venice*, for instance, the song the musicians sing in Belmont, just before Bassanio goes against appearances and chooses the leaden casket containing Portia's picture, makes clear that "concupiscence of the eye" leads to nothing valuable or lasting: "Tell me where is fancy bred?/Or in the heart or in the head?/How begot, how nourished?" And the reply gives us our estimate of appearances: "It is engendered in the eyes,/With gazing fed; and fancy dies/In the cradle where it lies." The song is a suggestion to the audience that Bassanio must use his imagination if he is to be successful in winning his lady. In *Cymbeline*, Imogen's husband Posthumus follows fancy in being deceived by the visual tokens of her boudoir brought to him by Iachimo, but later Imogen defines the right path of imagination by not entirely crediting the appearance of her husband's death in the figure of a headless corpse beside her in the grave, dressed in her husband's clothes. Imagination, in contrast to fancy, always involves an action of the heart: it never misses the mark.

According to Coleridge, the primary imagination, the agent of perception, undertakes a gathering in of material to make an image in the mind—a repetition of that eternal creation that is before us—investing perception with an element of meaning. Secondary imagination dissolves the first image and recreates it in order to accomplish a unity with the whole structure of meaning. This distinction represents an important milepost in literary and philosophical thought, as important to literary theory and perhaps as radical as Max Planck's to physics. Further, it is fully as significant for educational theory. Imagination is not limited to literature. And in educational thought, it is the primary imagination that is most neglected, in the interests of the secondary and shaping operations of innovation, ingenuity, and—finally—efficiency.

The primary imagination must function with a certain plenitude and waste—a redundancy—that tends to scandalize educational administrators. But redundancy, we might consider, has its own benefits; indeed, redundancy, rather than some such guide as Occam's razor, describes the essential path of imagination. The very concept of redundancy perhaps needs some rehabilitation in modernity, an age devoted to frugality and efficiency. Redundancy has been an indispensable feature of creativity in technology. When the Boeing 747 was in its testing period a top executive of one of the large aircraft manufacturing corporations allayed my dismay at the seeming vulnerability of so large a ship by informing me that because of its enormous redundancy, with four back-up arrangements for virtually every vital operation, it was the most invincible plane in the air—very nearly indestructible. Safety requires the deliberate building in of redundancy in a multitude of situations in which a failure could be lethal. Men are back from the moon because of redundancy. Nuclear reactors have avoided serious accidents because back-up devices have shut down the operation when primary controls failed. Not only safety but reliability requires this excess of equipment, this superabundance of possibilities. The telephone system has many paths by which one can get from here to New York. Sometimes, in our experience of small appliances—at home, in business, in cars—when something breaks, the entire apparatus stops. In the device itself redundancy is absent; economy and competition have demanded the most direct and somewhat marginal arrangement of design. And yet redundancy is still assumed, present in the person who uses the device—in us, if you will. When the blender refuses to whirl, we beat the egg with a fork, as in similar failures of technology we calculate percentages with pencil and paper; we call a taxi. *We* become part of the system.

Quite obviously I am speaking of the imagination, if at a rather mundane level. But it is true that in the face of an unexpected difficulty we do make a conscious movement of the will, review our memory, exercise prudence and judgment, and choose alternate paths. For the airplane, the spacecraft, the nuclear reactor, the telephone system, the unexpected must become pre-expected—the imagination must be cast into a "what-if" mode or, better, a "what-if-what-then?" mode. The designer of a product or a project faces our emergency for us. I suspect—or I might even say I imagine— that industry will give us more of this multiplicity in future products. The micro-processor fairly well assures redundancy, as do the increasing incidents of lawsuits. There are many reasons for providing alternate paths—versatility, precision, capacity, reliability, bounty—but in the end the marketplace will govern. Providing an excess will be a matter of style, of what appeals to the consumer. It gives one pause to think of what an ad writer could do with the slogan, "Redundancy—we've got it!"

The fact that love is redundant Elizabeth Barrett Browning told us some time ago. "Let me count the ways," she volunteered, but pretty well gave up on the task. But as she must have known, any relationship becomes more secure when the passageways of exchange multiply. Marriage is an excellent example: when one channel fails, another takes over the communication. A city is a very fragile structure if its members have only legal ties to one another. For the springs of life to flow, there need to be many communities within a city—not merely neighborhoods that federate in common interests but overlapping, superfluous communities with each person belonging to several—able to be reached by many pathways. Industries at times make the mistake of assuming that organization charts really define the flow of authority. The chart is merely a refuge of last resort; if a person's authority is solely derived from that thin line on the chart, someone else should be in his position. The authenticity of authority has many expressions. It, too, is redundant—versatile, able to abandon one procedure for another.

The imagination is the instrument of redundancy. It is the faculty that projects alternatives, creating acts of supererogation. This ability is engendered by a process that runs about as follows: phenomena in the world are taken into the mind through sensors, passed through what computer operators call the "rat file" of undifferentiated memory, then fed to the primary imagination. Here perception occurs. It may consist of recognition, of association, of differentiation, of characterization—such as lovely, delicate, gross, or horrible. Some sort of wholeness, some multiplicity and copiousness are ascribed to a phenomenon, making it an event. Any truth must be proved along the pulse, as Keats has written, insisting upon the wholeness of experience, its bodily aspects as well as its immaterial ones. One "feels" the truth of the experience, and in an age of abstraction, where this primary experience is largely lost, it is not surprising that poets have for some two centuries emphasized the heart and body more than the mind, that Keats' cry "O for a life of sensations rather than of thoughts!" is understandable. Sensations provide us with that superabundance of experience that gives us a sense of the "world's body."

I suspect the ineffable quality of taste is operative in the very process of perception—taste being, as I see it, discrimination, fidelity to the truth of the material taken in by the senses. (This *saltimbocca* is excellent, even if it was prepared at a small unpretentious *trattoria*. This dress is lovely, even if it was bought at a discount store.)

The question arises of whether taste can be taught. Without a doubt it can be simulated—that is, a person can acquire a catalog of things judged to be in good taste and then compare a new experience with the catalogued entities. But that sort of comparison, involving the setting up of standards and the acquisition of vast stores of information, is not the work of the imagination. It is instead a scholarly activity, an appeal to an outside authority, not to that inner awareness that inherently knows true from false. In all likelihood taste cannot be taught; but it can be awakened. Everyone no doubt has the capacity for good taste; but in many people that capacity is so crusted over with cliches of thought and convention that they cannot see an object for what it is in itself. They refuse to submit to its redundancy and complexity and thereby fail to bring taste into play. Admittedly, taste is a very complica ted faculty, accommodating itself to temporal style and yet having within it something constant above style that is uncompromising about quality. Taste is consequently hard to speak of or to teach. Further, any talk about taste always makes people restive. But I would nevertheless propose that taste is an aspect of the primary imagination, occurring for the most part in the act of perception, although at times the discrimination of taste may be deferred and handed over to judgment, something that lies in the secondary imagination, if I understand that distinction correctly.

The secondary imagination is more deliberate, more resourceful, more ingenious than the primary. It summons up the original perception, imposing a "credible order on ordinary reality," in Eliot's phrasing. It orders an appropriate action and places in the memory a record that can be recalled at will. The imagination thus becomes the avenue to learning.

But is there really any such faculty as the imagination? Can we point to any spot and say, there it is? Of course not. It is anywhere and everywhere, a sort of wave function that has its principal amplitude in the person. But it would be interesting to see if we can find some analogue for imagination in the human brain. Reality, we must remember, is only a metaphor for meaning, but the correspondences are enlightening. Consider the process of sight. A signal from the retina is brought to the back of the brain to a spot called the primary visual area; it then goes to the associated visual area—we might call it the secondary visual area—where it is processed in some fashion, registered in a short-term memory and sent on across the brain to initiate an appropriate action. The primary, the secondary, and the output—not a bad correspondence. Is that back part of the brain then the imagination? No, but it is part of its instrumentation and its metaphor. Coleridge's description somewhat anticipates by a hundred and fifty years the presently understood arrangement of visual perception.

The other senses, too, have their primary and secondary perception areas—sound, smell, and touch, or auditory, olfactory, and somatosensory. Each has its own memory. These, too, are part of the imagination's equipment; we might say that the imagination is redundant in its senses. It is like a dog that seeks to recognize its master by sight, sound, smell, and touch—by taste, too, if it can lick him. Like the dog, the imagination is goal-oriented. It seeks to know its object however it can and by as many ways as it can.

Another redundancy of the imagination lies in the two hemispheres of the brain. Each is capable, as the neurosurgeon J. E. Bogen tells us, "of functioning independently, each in a manner different from the other." Is it too unimaginative to look for a moment at that remarkable organ which has been slighted in the past three centuries by being reduced to pure matter? It seems a bit angelic of us not to acknowledge the stuff of which even dreams are made. However much we may wish to belong to the plane of pure thought, it is to the physical realm that the mortal condition pays homage. Gross as it may seem, not only movement, digestion, and growth, but every sensation, every emotion, every thought is accompanied by an exchange of energy in the subject organism.

Within the brain that energy is delivered by the blood—at least the oxygen needed for the reduction of glucose is so delivered. If we can see what part of the brain requires additional blood when any specific action is taking place, we can see what areas of the brain are associated with different actions. A group in Sweden and Denmark has carried on such a study over a score of years on some five hundred patients. These biophysicists infuse low-level radioactive xenon into the artery feeding certain sections of the brain, then take radiation scans as the subject rests or performs specified tasks. An increase of counting rate (in the radiation detector placed on a small area of the skull) indicates a greater xenon concentration, therefore more blood, more oxygen supply, more energy demand, more brain activity. Seeing an object at rest activates one area, its moving requires two more, reading still two more, and reading aloud another two. These areas are near the surface of the brain, since the radiation is of quite low energy and would not escape from the interior. The areas are specific to certain tasks. Much of the information thus gathered has also come from other studies—open brain surgery, in which the brain can be touched and corresponding motion observed; micro-electrode studies in which small signals can be inserted; radioactive oxygen uptake studies. The studies are consistent, able to be combined into a mapping of the cerebral cortex, all very much like the old phrenological diagrams in which the various bumps on the head indicate traits and abilities.

The cortex is a folded membrane covering virtually the whole top of the head from about the eyebrow to the back edge of the skull and from ear to ear, but very clearly divided into two hemispheres, the right half controlling the left side of body reactions, the left half the right side. The membrane is folded in such a way as to define quite clearly two rows that run from ear to ear circling a little back of the top of the skull, interrupted by the slight gulf between right and left hemispheres. The row nearer the front is the motor cortex: it sends signals to the hands and feet, telling them to move. Each spot controls a certain member and, one presumes, a certain kind of response.

The other row across the brain is the somatosensory (body-sensing) cortex, separated from the motor cortex by a crease in the membrane. It receives messages from the members— touches, heat, or shock, and programs a response which is fed across to the corresponding part of the motor cortex.

What I have been doing is imagining the brain—imagining in the sense of forming a mental image. It might have been helpful to have a diagram pointing out certain areas—or better yet, a model. If one had a biology department available, one could borrow the plaster cast of the brain, pick it up, look at it for a moment and, raising one's eyes, say, "Alas, poor Yorick, I knew him, Horatio." (Prufrock was wrong: we were *all* meant to be Hamlet.) The brain, I might note, is a more appropriate addressee than the skull for the question "Where be your jibes now?" Somewhere within the brain a scintillation accompanies every jest. I say "accompanies" because I need to emphasize that we do not know the origin of thought. We do not know where *will* resides or imagination dwells.

We can, however, locate some imagined acts—for instance, the act of reading silently. The visual message (of silent reading) activates not only the visual responses but also a speech-planning area, even though actual speaking does not occur. We do not know what the sequence would be had the reading merely been imagined; such a study was not done. But an imagined motor sequence has been tried: a subject was asked to imagine operating a typewriter. The supplementary motor area of the brain (the planning area for motion) became active, nothing else. We can suppose, then, that somewhere an anticipation area is activated by an imagined image, just as that little speech-planning area was active in silent reading.

Where do the images come from? How are they willed forth? Where is the memory? These questions may someday be identified with localized regions of the brain buried well beneath the cortex. But I would hazard a guess that particularities, individualities, specific thoughts and creativity occur in a realm forever concealed by a basic indeterminacy, something akin to Heisenberg's Uncertainty Principle. Science can carry us a long way, but inevitably it reaches an impenetrable mystery—not merely a lack of precise instrumentation but a fundamental limitation on knowledge about existence, about what I choose to call this created universe.

But let me return for a moment to that little speech-planning area. It exists in *both* hemispheres of the brain, as if we had two tongues to tell, and both are activated in imagining. But the one on the left, known as Broca's area, is the only necessary one. If it is destroyed in a person by an accident, he cannot speak, though otherwise unimpaired. The right member, however, may be destroyed with no observable effect. Another special area in the left side of the auditory associate area pertains to the comprehension of hearing. In the light of these findings, some justification exists for thinking of the left hemisphere as the acoustic side of the brain and, by symmetry, the right side as visual.

This dualistic apprehension of the world became the chief interest of Marshall McLuhan in his last years. Earlier, McLuhan had given all of us who followed his thought in such books as *The Gutenberg Galaxy* and *Understanding Media* an ability to see things in a different light—pattern recognition, he called it. He was a seer, one who could spread a vision of the future, not in terms of its coming events, but in terms of its evolving modes of thought and imagination. His interest in the brain extended the same concerns. Despite many factual inaccuracies, what he provided is a picture of two world sensibilities, one linear, sequential, logical, and active; the other spatial, simultaneous, intuitive, and reflective. Out of this dichotomy civilizations emerge—the West on the left, the Orient on the right. The holistic right plays *ground* to the specialized left *figure*. All this is a myth, certainly, rather than a factual account, but it is illuminating and provocative.

What I have been indicating is that learning as I conceive it is not a highly efficient operation. It is not a matter of determining which explanation is most direct, what minimum number of experiments need be performed. Instead, a certain richness, a multiplicity of possibilities, a fine excess are required if the imagination is to be instructed properly. At times a mentor must forbid the easy path for his student in order that the surrounding territory be explored. A tight wire may be the shortest path between two points, but it is not the most easily travelled. The shortest, straightest path may have its own hazards. There comes a time when a lion is in the path; then the long way round is best.

The imagination builds its resources not so much from the memory of specific instances as from general principles that are the distillation of particularities—the conservation of energy, for example. But even such principles are not simple keys to problems. They are aids to orientation within situations, ways toward knowing—not the knowing itself. Knowing is full-bodied, massive, a dark tower; and once Childe Roland has followed the crooked path to knowledge, he may survey the surrounding terrain and discover any number of redundant service roads that lead to the same territory.

One might say that knowing is always particular, a knowing of one thing. Understanding is more general; it places the particular in a class, the class of things that are similarly understood. Knowing is outward-directed, understanding is inward-directed. Imagination is the faculty that mediates this process: it takes a full-bodied, copious image of the object, puts it in order, and presents it to the understanding. An act of the imagination is always a learning event. Even when it is acting without outside information, forming its images purely from internal resources, in an active planning session or in quiet contemplation, the imagination presents new material to the understanding in a copiousness of joy.

Can learning occur by some path other than the imagination? Undoubtedly we learn our multiplication tables—or did before the hand-held calculator—by rote, by repetition, with little imagination. Skills quite generally come through some kind of programming procedure. Is the computer made in our image, or vice versa? We say we put the computer in a "learning mode," a term borrowed from our side of the ledger giving the machine some human dignity, and we say that we are "programmed" for skills, a computer term reducing us to the level of the machine. Behavioral learning is related to this programming, perhaps in the manner of the smart computers that teach themselves—that is, adjust their own controls in order to behave according to predetermined standards. Understanding is not obtained by such a process in man or machine. In justice to behavioral psychology, I should say that many of its adherents do have an implicit faith that, for some subjects, understanding will rise out of behavior—not for most people, true, but enough to supply the necessary in‑ novation and creativity a society requires. Such "sports," as we may call them, would not likely occur with computers, but I am not yet prepared to say how far the development of arti‑ ficial intelligence is apt to be carried. The aim in that branch of technology is to develop a computer that can perfect its own knowledge—expand its capacity and refine its ways of handling all levels of information. Several generations of computers may be required to achieve the purpose, but what should result finally is the super‑computer, smarter and faster than all mankind. Along with many other computer experts, Joseph Weizenbaum has expressed alarm at the progress being made toward this development of artificial intelligence. A veritable cult has grown up among programmers, he says, who take their mission as religious in their devotion to the new creation they consider the step above man in the evolu‑ tionary scheme. Their goal, he maintains, is to reach world supremacy in twenty years—2001. But, whatever dangers we may face from these innovations, we can be absolutely certain that the computer, refined to its ultimate, can never develop an imagination. It may not need to. Power is inherently brutish. The computer is a willing slave: how kind a master it will be is questionable.

But the take-over may not be as imminent as the cult wor‑ shippers suppose. There is an asymptotic development to all stable enterprises—a very rapid rise at the beginning, then a gradual bending over, with the curve never quite reaching theideal state. It is quite likely that artificial intelligence is self-limiting. In its terms, what it can learn is of the same order as the material it learns from.

In view of the widespread conception of "learning" as any alteration of method in handling information—by computers as well as people—it may perhaps be capricious to reserve the term for the process of acquiring understanding. But although data, information, analysis, scholarship, and criticism may present themselves at the door of understanding, only imagination opens that door. And the operation of the imagination, as I have indicated, requires redundancy.

The condemnatory connotations carried by that word, however, are not of so long standing as one might suppose. *Redundancy* comes from the Latin *re* (an intensive) plus *dundare* to swell, surge, as a wave. In the English language it had the meaning of *copiousness, fullness of being, plenteousness, bountifulness, superabundance, amplification, overflowing*; and only after the influence of Occam's razor and Peter Ramus's logic did it begin to take on the connotations of *excess, superfluity, repetition, more than enough*, and, finally, *unnecessary* and *wasteful*. The modern goals of efficiency and productivity would eliminate this superabundance, not only in production but, more ominously, in education and culture itself. Let us hope that situation is, indeed, changing. The fullness of the imagination, of creativity, can exist in culture only with many possible alternatives, allowing duplication and the free play of imagination.

I do not mean to be saying, however, that the person of imagination must persist in walking down all possible different paths. The liberal arts have always been thought of as ways to knowledge, not methods; and, as Cardinal Newman wrote, learners need to be taken to a high hill to survey the surrounding countryside if they are to have any notion of the scope of knowledge. Once they have seen the multifariousness, the redundancy of the landscape and the paths winding about in it, they can never forget that glimpse. It is the very uniqueness of a liberal education that it affords such a view, making use of imagination and not analysis as its moving power.

But I would be deceptive if I did not acknowledge that exclusion is as important to the imagination as inclusion. "Two roads diverged in a yellow wood,/And sorry I could not travel both/And be one traveler. . . . /I took the one less traveled by. . . . " We know about the roads; we respect those who travel either. And we know there are roads beyond these roads, unseen. But for oneself, one takes the road less traveled by, or perhaps the other; or one keeps searching for an alternate route. But if we are to enter the dark woods— with its copiousness, its overwhelming fullness, its plenitude, its redundancy—each of us must finally choose one path, straight, narrow, and severe.

8

The Uncertainty Principle in Education

THE CHANCES that two particular people, say you and I, out of all the possible configurations of matter, should here be in communication are, as a recent cartoon strip informed us, infinitesimal—about one in 33 zillion. (Someone has recently announced the discovery of the largest number yet conceivable—the killion. It will kill you if you see it written out.) But here we are—not a probability at all. As of this moment, the chances are a hundred percent certain that we *are* here. By such paradoxes the Uncertainty Principle speaks truth.

The Uncertainty Principle (for I am going to use that epoch-making discovery as a fundamental metaphor for my remarks) is also known as the Indeterminacy Principle—two sides of the same coin, Uncertainty and Indeterminacy—the Tweedledee and Tweedledum of twentieth-century epistemology. Uncertainty is a condition of *knowing* (on the part of an observer); indeterminacy is a condition of *being*—on the part of an object observed, not merely in our formulation of what is being observed, but in the thing itself. Now in concerning myself with the relation between education and this insight into the limitations of knowledge, I mean to explore the indeterminacy of *things*, the inherent range of freedom that things have in their interaction with one another, and to see how that indeterminacy affects the entire process of education.

In order to understand the dominant figure for my metaphor, let us see how clearly we can bring into focus the Principle of Uncertainty. In the description of how a physical system works—a checker sliding across a slanted board, for instance—there is a property called "action" that is the product of *momentum* and *distance*. Momentum is composed of body and speed—the mass of a body times its velocity. Since the checker will be both pulled by gravity and slowed by friction, its momentum is likely to be different, greater or lesser, along each little interval of path length. Projecting the checker horizontally across the board, we can visualize it as it slows down because of friction but then picks up speed as gravity accelerates it down the slope. The checker traces out a curving path on the slanting board. To arrive at the total action, one would have to add up all the products of momentum and distance over each little interval of path length— integrate it, we could say if we are free to use the calculus. Now if we can visualize different curved courses the checker might take on its way down, it should seem reasonable that the total action would be different for different paths taken.

The actual path the checker chooses, we should be happy to learn, is the one that has the least total action. That phenomenon is the result of a general economy observed by nature. It might seem more reasonable to say the path chosen is the one that loses least energy to friction. This is a valuable principle to know, this "least action." It predicts how physical things will operate, how natural things behave.

We have said that any action is the product of momentum and distance—of the mass and speed of a body times the distance it traverses. Distance is the space travelled—an interval between two positions. In any action, then, momentum (a body property) and position (a space property) are what we call conjugate variables, canonically conjugate, we say— joined together by law for the sake of this variational principle of least action. Energy and time are similarly conjugate

—similarly wedded—working together to serve the same magnificent economy of nature.

In the old Newtonian physics—that comfortable, mechanistic, highly determined world in which we grew up, only recently superseded—these little intervals of action that must be added together could be as small as we liked, could, in fact, be infinitesimals. But in 1901, at the beginning of the twentieth century, Max Planck disturbed that comfortable security. He found it necessary to introduce what he called the quantum of energy in order to explain the variation of color intensity emitted by the sun. An oscillator at any one frequency, he said, could have energies only in multiples of h times the frequency; and h, Planck's constant, as it came to be known, was seen to be the smallest possible unit of our old friend, *action*. Planck, Einstein, and others, principally Bohr (who recognized that angular momentum was itself action), showed conclusively that action does not change smoothly, continuously, but only in jumps of h.

That realization has given us our concept of the atom and of all its constituents—the leptons and six quarks out of which all things are made. In a descending order, three quarks are bound together by gluons into protons and neutrons, these bound together by pions into nucleons, these by photons to electrons to make up the chemical elements, which join to form molecules—and eventually, as we have already noted, you and I confront each other. So, at least, goes our present myth.

In contemplating the unit of action, Heisenberg recognized in 1927 that basic uncertainty exists in our knowledge of the physical world. It is only by observation that we can evaluate such quantities as energy and time or momentum and position—and Heisenberg's startling insight is that every observation has an inherent uncertainty characteristic of the medium used for the measurement. Position of a particle, for example, can be determined only within a wavelength of the light used for observation. If we change to shorter wavelength, say an x-ray, we can decrease the uncertainty of position, but this more energetic x-ray would transfer its momentum to the particle in an unspecified direction and thus increase the uncertainty in momentum. Hence a reciprocity exists in which two conjugate variables increase or diminish in relation to each other, with the total product remaining constant. The uncertainty in our knowledge of *position* times the uncertainty in our knowledge of *momentum* can never be less than Planck's constant, so Heisenberg showed. We can never know a physical event with more certainty than h. We are similarly limited in our knowledge of energy and time. Einstein commented on this world-shaking discovery: "It was as if the ground had been pulled out from under one, with no firm foundation to be seen anywhere upon which one could build."

Gradually, however, it has come to be realized that these discoveries have themselves constituted a new foundation. This principle of reciprocity and the other principle I have already mentioned—that any observation disturbs the thing observed—are two aspects of the Uncertainty Principle that make it pregnant with possibilities for analogy. And herein is its supreme cultural significance. Before this time, Western civilization had worked within the idea of opposites—viewing experience in terms of polarities: black and white, earth and sky, male and female, nature and culture, good and evil. Two poles were regarded as pulling in opposite directions, so that the different forces worked against each other, and any achievement was made in the tension between the two extremes. This balance of opposites has governed the Western mind. Aristotle's "Golden Mean," considered to be the path of the virtuous man, was conceived of as the happy medium between excess and defect—rashness as excess, for example, and cowardice as defect. In between lies courage. In the new physics, which is radically altering the Western imagination, the two conjugate variables are not opposites, but, like Yin and Yang, reciprocals in their ability to be known exactly, working together like a married couple, each supplementing the other's deficiencies, neither trying to overcome the other and assume dominance.

One further aspect of Indeterminacy should be mentioned. We have had to recognize that this principle of uncertainty represents a barrier to our desire to know. "Ah, what a dusty answer gets the soul/When hot for certainties in this our life," George Meredith laments in his sonnet sequence "Modern Love." And the dusty answer is not due to our own inept methods—which might be correctable—nor our own obtuse instruments—which might be perfectible. It is nature herself that lowers the gate when we are "hot for certainties." But under the amazing generosity in which we live, where nature closes one road, she opens another. Within the realm of indeterminacy, one discovers, the imagination has free play, as it did not have in a strictly predictable universe. Within this "dark interval" of unknowability, this fundamental unit of action, imagination is free until it hits the wall— from the inside. Outside the wall that marks the observable world, energy is conserved and must be audited and accounted for; inside, energy can be created at will, *ex nihilo*, out of nothing, provided the time during which this energy exists respects Planck's constant. It is somewhat like the McCaslin slaves in Faulkner's *Go Down, Moses*, who can slip out the back door after dark and roam the countryside freely, provided they are back inside by dawn. Millions of possible worlds can come into being; and until we know how things do turn out, they have their own multiple scenarios of possibility.

The making of such scenarios is a virtual process, not actual in the sense of existing outside the limits of the uncertainty interval. Elementary-charged particles, that are no more than points, for example, can emit virtual photons which can in turn change themselves to virtual pairs of charges, forming a sheath around the original point charge, like Cinderella's coach that must be back in the pumpkin patch—that is, reabsorbed—by its appointed time. Another coach is then formed to replace it. Virtual particles cannot, of course, be seen. They remain imaginary until such time as a prediction requiring their presence results in a real observation. And yet something can be clarified in this realm and carried back to the ordered world, much as the participants in A Midsummer Night's Dream, carry back wisdom to Athens. It may be that the mass and size of real particles are of this nature. The secrets of the universe may dwell within the bulwarks of indeterminacy, this great fecund matrix of things, penetrable only by the free play of the imagination.

So much for my principal figure of thought. We can begin my main concern—education—with a somewhat formidable definition, formidable because I am here attempting to include in one statement all the qualifying aspects of this crucially important endeavor of our society.

Education is a formal process of synthetic learning in which symbolic material is organized into a skeletal structure; on this structure learning from experience accumulates in such a fashion that meaning is drawn from extended areas of the structure.

Now let me analyze this statement. Education is a process, a sequence of operations headed toward a definite end. It is a formal process, following rules and established forms; thus it implies a social function, an activity duly authorized by society, guided by professional authorities, and undertaken in an orderly fashion. The process is synthetic learning, an artificial action, requiring an artfully designed, purposeful amalgamation of selected material. The entire *praxis* is symbolic, in that what is learned comes to stand for more than itself, to suggest intangible and universal ideas, moving always toward contemplation. In the operation, concrete and individual instances suggest larger entities, by means of metaphoric,

synechdochic, or elliptical modes of thought. Metaphor con-
nects one body of material with another, the intellect bridg-
ing a gap by the discernment of similarities. Synechdoche
takes the part for the whole, calling up an intuition of order
and harmony; ellipsis engages an incomplete figure that must
be filled in by an imagination of unity if one is to apprehend
the entire pattern. These tropological processes are more
than figures of speech; they are figures of thought, the means
by which the intellect intuitively apprehends meaning.

With this analysis in hand, we are saying that education
makes use of carefully and economically selected data pur-
posefully arranged to indicate the whole of reality, working
by condensation, compression, incompleteness, suggestion.
The end point of the process is the organizing of this material
into a structure in the minds of students, a logical framework
within which a student may reason from point to point. The
structure is to be such as to provide an addressable place for
true learning to reside, whenever it is acquired. Meaning, so
the definition implies, exists in the relationships of these
various nodules of learning. There it is. Education is a formal
process of synthetic learning wherein symbolic material is
organized into a significant structure.

But something about all this is unsatisfactory. This definition, though a serious attempt to look at the educational
process afresh, seems nevertheless a bit irrelevant, perhaps
outmoded, in its logical abstraction. The fact of its being old-
fashioned, however, does not invalidate its distinctions. The
features named are principles to which teachers and academic
administrators must return periodically in order to solidify
the enterprise in which they are engaged. From time to time it
must be clarified that education is a symbolic process: it is not
the gathering of information; it is not life itself: it is an art
form, requiring skill in design and skill in performance, pointing toward understanding. From time to time we must
remember that education and learning are not synonymous,

that education takes place in a highly limited arena at a crucial stage of life and that learning, once initiated, is a continuous process.

We might notice the predominantly spatial sense in which this definition is framed. Education in its interstices is spatial. And, indeed, education as an activity occurs in a restricted space and is socially directed—a communal affair. Learning, on the other hand, is quite a different activity. It is informal, natural, concerned with actual things, loosely organized in such a fashion that meaning is local and specific. It is a lifelong pursuit, internally directed, and intensely personal.

With our minds ripe for analogy, doubtless we tend to match up conjugate variables—not, let me caution you, education and learning. I am not about to say that they are reciprocals—that the more we have of one, the less we have of the other (the more education, the less learning and vice versa—though cracker-box philosophy of the Will Rogers variety has long had it so). Of course education and learning are related, quite intimately, just as are momentum and energy, but they are independent in the mathematical sense of being of different degrees, in the sense that x is of first degree, x^2 is of second. Momentum is conjugate to position, energy is conjugate to time.

It might be helpful to set up *momentum* as counterpart for education and *energy* as counterpart for learning. Momentum, the analogue for education, is of first degree in velocity. The product of mass and velocity, it is a vector, heading in a certain direction with a certain speed, holding the property of inertia, or resistance to forces that would change its direction or speed. Energy, on the other hand, is half the mass times velocity *squared*—second degree. One should note that this kinetic energy, is only *part* of a body's possible energy, just as the learning that one does in school through education is only part of possible learning. A body has, as well, potential energy by virtue of its interaction with environment and inherent energy by virtue of its *being*—its rest mass times the velocity of light squared, $E = mc^2$, as Einstein pointed out. Energy is a scalar property, without sense of direction. It simply has magnitude, a total amount of energy that belongs to the body in question, though some energy may lie in the surrounding region. Like the mind's apprehension of truth, which occurs in learning, energy is a cosmic property, permeating the entire universe—changeable, moving, an aspect of existence itself.

The terms of our analogy now become apparent. Like momentum, education is first order; it is the thing one is doing while one is doing it. It has a direct, vector-like quality about it. Education is conjugate to—is joined to—*space* in this analogical scheme of things. Its spaces are the campus, the laboratory, the classroom. And in this relation to space is to be found the reciprocity arrangement of conjugates. Education intensifies as space diminishes. In the broad stretches of existence, in life generally, education diminishes to a level of non-existence. Only a deliberate return to the semblance of a classroom for an hour, an evening, a weekend can again institute education.

Learning is second degree and exceeds education, as x^2 is of a higher order of being than x. Learning is done while one is really doing something else. It is a received quality, something possessed, not going anywhere, the scalar product of vectors. Like energy, learning is conjugate with time. The times of learning are life time, job time, schooling time, the academic year, the semester, the class period, the conference. And again, as the time span shortens, learning intensifies.

All of this schematization is little more than an ingenious metaphor or a kind of metaphysical conceit, one might be justified in saying: that is, one might charge that I have extended a limited analogy between two areas so far that it is made to represent a purported total similarity. And so I no doubt have. But the virtue of a metaphorical expedition is the realignment of the landscape when viewed through various exaggerations and distortions. The salient features become well separated. It is at least for some of us instructive to distinguish education and learning as sharply as this approach demands. Any battle against behaviorism, any disdain for mnemonic learning must then stand in review, particularly if one's own mode of instruction seeks always to engender insight. "See, see," one shouts, and occasionally someone does. And that look of joy on a single face is sufficient reward to reinforce belief in one's method. But now, as we view the educational process through the present set of analogies, we must grant the efficacy of mundane instruction, the patient construction of the logical framework for knowledge. It is the same framework for the whole class, a framework that will perdure in the enveloping society. *The construction of that framework is the business of education.* Otherwise the acquisition of knowledge becomes mere information-gathering. The relation of such a frame to learning is the making of a habitat, a nesting place for insights which will come, willy-nilly, when they choose.

Insights are those intense experiences of learning that occur in brief moments, in flashes, one by one to each person individually. Education does contribute to learning—synthetic learning, I have called it—but, just as for energy, two other sources exist for learning: experience that, like potential energy, is an interaction with environment; and instinctive knowledge that, like rest mass energy, comes with existence itself. It seems that insights should happen more frequently in the precious educational space than in the outside world; but whether they develop then or years later, they come to the person, not to the class. Education supplies only a portion of learning. Its function is not so much to supply learning as to ready people for the task of learning.

Learning and insight give rise to joy and a suffusion of beauty, whereas education yields at most satisfaction. Or so I should conclude in looking back over the *schema* I have set up for education. But I am not content with so much humble pie; such deprecation does not really square with the experience of teaching. The definition set forth for education is undoubtedly right and the analysis correct. But something is amiss. It may be that the analogies employed need more careful analysis.

Perhaps the very term *analysis* supplies the key to the outmodedness of my definition. Such a scheme as my proposed definition of education fairly begs for analysis. But, as we know from other evidence, the age of analysis is over. In separating the parts of the process so absolutely, I have been putting new insights into old methodologies. The result is not so much wrong as irrelevant—old-fashioned. Such a procedure is a reduction of a vital body into its parts. And, as we all know, one does not tell time by taking the watch apart. For a good while now, meaning has not been sought in analysis, not really even in synthesis, but in a quest for unity. Indeed, the mark of twentieth-century thought is this quest. The century began with Planck's constant and Einstein's relativity, two developments that shook apart the certainty that seemed immediately ahead. Einstein's effect was more immediate. Back in the eighteenth century, Isaac Newton had said, "Absolute space, in its own nature, without regard to anything external, remains always similar and immovable." And further, "Absolute, true, and mathematical time, of itself and by its own nature, flows uniformly, without regard to anything external." Einstein destroyed both of these absolutes. We can perhaps be spared the development of the rationale that allows space to shrink and time to expand with the increase in relative velocity between thing and observer. Our inevitable incredulity at such a phenomenon is no doubt mitigated when we remember that one of the consequences of this development is $E = mc^2$, which, in our time, has proved wholly and catastrophically believable. Now, can this destruction of absolutes be a step toward unity? Indeed it can. The theory is based on the proposition that all observers, anywhere in the universe, regardless of their states of motion, have equal access to nature's laws. That idea of universal equality, with its many analogues in politics, philosophy, and literary criticism, has thoroughly pervaded society with profound effects that are still working their way out and that will eventually change not only education but the encompassing style of our culture.

Education has been affected in ways much more subtle than the imposition of equal opportunity laws. The very stance of education has been shifting. A longstanding concern of some physicists has been finding a way to teach physics so that women can perform in this science as well as their male counterparts do. Of all the disciplines, physics most markedly demonstrates this strange imbalance between the sexes. Most women, quite simply, are not very much attracted to the analytic method. Nor, in truth, are some men. Perhaps a beginning for an alternative approach may be found, at least at the level of the non-science major, by starting with the myth of creation (the "big bang"), employing the very latest ideas of particle physics, as it is presented in the professional journals, then slowly increasing the quantitative content. If that strategy does not work, then some other one must, since the age demands equality. In the past we have begun logically with the simplest and most boring ideas—inclined planes, pulleys, bouncing balls—expecting to build up a quantitative competency adequate for advanced ideas. This method is like expecting Ferdinand to hew wood and draw water before he has ever seen Miranda—or making Dante undergo his laborious climb through the cosmos without ever having seen the face of Beatrice. We have to let him at least peek. What must be held up in the early stages is a vision of completeness splendid in its universality.

What I am saying is that education in our time needs to

desert the outmoded analytic approach and move toward a holistic concern, even in mathematical physics. Throughout the entire curriculum we need to readjust our stance, not through sentimental condescension, but through a frank and imaginative reseeing of our disciplines in their most fundamental aspects. Those of us who profess a discipline need to meld with it, go where it wants to go, let it, like the checker, choose the path of least action, lose the least energy to friction. We need to trust it. In new soil our discipline will likely blossom anew.

Equality, of course, is not unity but a precondition for it. Einstein undertook a unified field theory that would coalesce gravity and electromagnetism but could never work it out. Indeed, not long after his work, two more fundamental forces were discovered—increasing the number from two to four— the weak and the strong nuclear forces being added to electromagnetism and gravity. And recently a fifth was reported, which may or may not turn out to be actual, the evidence for or against its reality being yet inconclusive. Nonetheless, real progress has been made toward unity, largely through the agency of the now familiar Indeterminacy Principle, somewhat in the manner I have indicated. Of the four forces, however—gravity, electromagnetism, the weak force, and the strong—the middle two, as recent theory has shown, were originally unified as the electro-weak force, and the strong force is about to join them in a General Unified Theory, or GUT, as it is called.

Physics seems to be conducted in a high glee that recognizes the essential comic nature of the universe—and recognizes, too, that language, being metaphoric, is a fundamentally comic device. For the most part physicists' naming of things is innocent and juvenile, as in calling a nucleonic-sized area of 10^{-24}cm^2 a "barn." Occasionally, however, the designations are literary, as when Gell-Mann, in 1963, determining that protons and neutrons and other more fleeting heavy particles were not themselves elementary but were made up of three truly elementary particles, named these new particles "quarks." He had in mind a passage in Joyce's *Finnegan's Wake* where the bartender sings out "Three quarks for Mr. Mork." Quarks, as I mentioned, are held together by gluons, the whimsy constituting quite serious good fun.

Now the GUT is not really general, since it does not include gravity. The theory that does include gravity is called the TOE, the Theory of Everything, but thus far it is only a name. Gravity has resisted a quantization that would make gravitons as real as photons. Somehow, somewhere, the barriers to unity will be breached. The search for unity is the motion of our time, and physics is but a flagbearer in a general cultural surge.

Education, being a social institution, is always a little conservative, always dragging a bit; but, as we noticed before, it has picked up the strain of universal equality that Relativity bequeaths us. Some academic disciplines—physics, literature, art, psychology, perhaps even mathematics and philosophy—have begun that coupling of conjugates, that unity through reciprocity that the Uncertainty Principle outlines. It is as always a brave new world where the imagination is free within its limits to weave its magic and to let the formal process of education, as well as the passionately individual pursuit of learning, discover the joy and beauty of unity.

9

The Purpose of Educational Institutions

THE PRINCIPAL TASK of education is to prepare the society of twenty to forty years ahead. That span of years is about the time that will elapse before students now in college will be in charge of things—the time when their taste and judgment will shape economic and cultural life. If we accept the implications of this statement, it should be obvious that the purpose of education is not to prepare the young for immediate usefulness in society as we know it. As it turns out, well-educated persons are useful precisely because they have not been narrowly trained for a particular job; but that usefulness is, in a sense, simply a fortunate by-product of education. Neither is the purpose of education to perfect the individual in his enjoyment of life or even in his spiritual development. Though intimate and interior in its effect, education is social in its aims, too valuable and expensive by far to be a personal ornament. It is sponsored by society and carried on for its own purposes, although those purposes may be only dimly perceived.

These two deviations—utilitarianism and personalism—are the Scylla and Charybdis of education, the rock and the whirlpool, between which schools must steer with steady hand if they are to accomplish their principal task. The proper kind of education, what we call liberal education, is not to be aligned with either of these two frequently encountered alternatives. Nor is it a mixture or compromise between the two. A proper education must be thought out on its own terms with its territory clearly in view—society as it will be twenty to forty years ahead. That society does not yet exist, cannot be known or predesigned. It will be constructed by these students now under tutelage. We can think back over the past score of years and reflect on how much the character of these years is the product of the graduates of the forties—not their technical abilities so much as their taste and judgment. We could go on to relate the sober seventies to the depression days of the thirties and the turbulent sixties to the flaming twenties, but it might be better not to formulate too strict a cyclical view of history. Rather, perhaps something closer to Ortega's theory of generations would satisfy us: "A generation is an integrated manner of existence," he writes, "a fashion in living, which fixes itself indelibly on the individual." Generations share a general date and space, a period. At a certain point in a young person's life, Ortega continues, he is marked by the "men who represent the maturity of that period and who act as the administrators of that period in all its categories—in the universities, the newspapers, the government, in literary and artistic life." Since a human being is a "world-making animal," the world of each person is shaped (before he begins his own world-making) by the imaginative visions of the most influential people within a certain time-span. "The concept of the generations, converted into a method of historic investigation, consists in nothing more than projecting that structure across the past."

Something does shape the young at a particular time, and the imprint that is then given persists throughout the history of a particular age group. The Jane Fondas of the world will always be rebels (even when they are making a fortune in video instruction), and though we may come to view them in their maturity with more understanding, tolerance, and even fondness, they retain their characteristic orientation toward the world. This outlook is not, I think, fatalistic. We are none of us determined by huge impassive forces against which we are helpless. We have free will and choice, can rise above environments and transcend barriers. But there is a period in each of our lives when sensibilities become set, after which our fundamental point of view rarely changes. The college years constitute that period—a time when the plasticity of youth is molded into its persistent form, when a permanent impression is made, when the bond issued at birth is renewed and signed under new terms. Any preparation of the future, as we can see, does indeed demand formation of the individual. A person must be elevated, his soul magnified, if he is to construct future society and move it toward those high aims that, though never fully achieved, impel civilization toward the good.

And yet, as I have emphasized, education is not a personal matter, not aimed at an individual's perfection of himself. In it the self must be progressively set aside. What T. S. Eliot said about the necessary loss of personality on the part of the poet applies as well to a genuine learner. The Christian paradoxes operate in education: attainment through abnegation, wisdom through ignorance, triumph through submission. Deliberately to choose abnegation, submission, and ignorance, however—to strive toward them—is to fall into their opposites, as the attempt to be humble tends to be an act of pride. Something of interest must be set up outside students, something that causes them to forget themselves and exist in that outside phenomenon. But here again the paradox is at work. If the professor designs the object for the purpose of making students forget themselves, at a certain point they will realize the trickery of the situation and join in or else reject the programmed response. Either way, the result is a trivialization of education. The learning process demands like the Greek goddesses a constant renewal of virginity. A good teacher will forget himself in the object, will pursue it with delight and surprise in the ever-recurring freshness, the eternal springtime of learning.

That approach to learning is the essence of a liberal education, as John Henry Newman admirably set forth in his *Idea of a University* a hundred years ago. The choice of subject matter is of little consequence, he said; it is the attitude toward it that makes a study liberal or servile. And when he described the liberal attitude as a pursuit of knowledge for its own sake, he implied that knowing is the chief joy, the chief "play," of human life.

Of course subject matter is of intense concern in the construction of a curriculum. A great tradition of learning exists in the West, wherein certain documents in literature, philosophy, politics, history, and theology are the common property of all educated persons. These texts have been made so by their power to transform souls and guide whole groups of people toward public virtues: honor, courage, magnanimity, civility. Such documents are not relics of the past, historic mementoes of bygone achievements, but affirmations as fully current now in their formative power as they were when freshly minted.

The King James Bible was once the principal document of American society. It formed the intellect, will, and imagination of an entire people. It shaped our language, providing metaphors, phrases, and typologies for daily life. Everyone, even the most illiterate, shared that language, so that resonances were set up by certain phrases—*the substance of things hoped for, whited sepulchres, sounding brass and tinkling cymbals*, for example. Sometime in the 1950's, as one could tell in the classroom, those resonances died out; and society, much the poorer for it, has lost a bond between its members. That loss is part of a general transfer of responsibility from home and church to school. In the great American experiment, as it might still be called, everyone has a high-school education and more than half at least some college study. This remarkable attempt at universal schooling has destroyed forever any elitist taint to education. The danger in shaping an entire nation by a school system, however, is that with an inadequate curriculum the binding ideals, images, and language of a whole people could be forgotten. The schools, particularly colleges and universities, need to be certain that they re-forge the bonds of community by bringing life and currency to the fundamental documents on which our society is based. And those documents are not a limited set of select political texts but an entire cultural heritage.

This heritage is a flexible, multifaceted medium as it exists now through a recapitulation of "the best that has been thought and said." In one sense, education is an intimacy with the great minds that have gone before us. Plato becomes one of our friends; we know how he thinks and we know how differently his pupil Aristotle views the world. The gnarled, brilliant mind of Saint Paul falls open to us, as does the mind and heart of his follower, several centuries later, Saint Augustine. In contrast, we do not know the minds of artists— of Homer or Shakespeare or Faulkner; rather, we know their creations, Achilles and Odysseus, Hamlet and Lear, Gavin Stevens and Flem Snopes. We know them not only in the context of artifacts, but also in the imaginative realm in which those characters exist. By means of the activated imagination engendered by the work of art, we see the metaform behind the entire body of the artist's vision. In another sense than this intimacy, however, education is an overview, as we occasionally withdraw a bit to take on an historical perspective. We see the overthrow of the Titans by the Olympians or hear Yahweh through the ears of Moses and the Prophets. We witness the recovery of Greek art and thought by Renaissance humanists and view the vast geographical explorations of their compeers. This awareness of participating in events that took place in another epoch, of coming to know persons who have been long dead, of experiencing ideas from the past as though they have just been conceived, is the necessary attitude of a liberal education, the only effective way to preserve a cultural heritage in memory and thus insure its life in the present.

That the concern of liberal learning is the present, not the past, is perhaps most apparent in the natural sciences. Admittedly, these studies have histories, even at times fascinating ones, that tell us much about the society in which certain discoveries were made; they reveal much, too, about the nature of the human mind. But historical studies contribute virtually nothing to scientific thought itself, at least not to science as it has defined itself in modernity. Science as science discards its artifacts as quickly as the concept involved is absorbed into the current community of its practitioners. It is a discipline that has agreed to surmount history, pointing beyond any single instance of itself to a total structure outside time. Attempts have been made from time to time to humanize science in the curriculum by presenting it through historical documents or biographies, but such attempts usually turn out to be exercises in futility. Science remains primitive, firsthand, with a kind of Edenic innocence and delight in the immediate revelations of nature. Any devotee can ascend to a glimpse of its total terrain, even though he would need a lifetime's work to be at home there. It is true that thus far scientists have done a rather poor job of conveying this experience to a wide spectrum of students, but in principle science is an essential part of a full education, important as a mode of thought that is universal in its implications.

A large body of work exists, then, in the disciplines indicated, as well as in economics and the visual, tactile, and temporal arts, making a dense fabric of meaning available to all educated persons. And, to pursue my metaphor, a proper educational scheme constantly cuts and shapes this fabric, making of it a garment suited to each new generation. This intricate fitting process is accomplished in a core curriculum which should be required of every student. In this way a rich set of references makes for communication of some subtlety and profundity between persons in widely diverse professions. Despite the complexity of society, its members are thus bonded together with shared ideals and images. To provide this common sense, these connective strands, is an educational task of no little urgency.

But this broad preparation of the core curriculum does not complete the task of liberal education in forming those who are to continue the never-ending work of building society. It would be a benefit for each person to go further and take on a chief mode of imagination, a chosen manner of viewing reality; but even more is it essential for a leader to do so. A person moves ahead in depth of thought by accepting and submitting to a major discipline—literature, philosophy, physics, history, and so on. The names of these subject matters may vary; new perspectives may lend their material to the disciplinary approach. But, though the varieties are infinite, actually only a handful of major "paths" provide access to the *speculum mentis*, the map of human wisdom. It is hard to say whether a student chooses a discipline or the discipline chooses the student. Some compatibility must exist between the mind and the mode of thought. This affinity is not due primarily to talent; in fact, talent is the most frequent cause of a mismatch. But usually, in some mysterious way, compatibility between person and discipline occurs. The student becomes imbued with a particular way of knowledge, forgets himself in it, and discovers his own originality and responsibility in its context.

A discipline is not, as we can see, a profession. A profession should be assumed in graduate school or in the school of the world. Many times during life a person may change his profession, but rarely does he change his discipline, his basic way of viewing things. This discipline, which may or may not have been his major in undergraduate college, provides his outlook in his professional work, supported by whatever technical training and expansion he has had. The discipline may relate to a chosen profession, as biology does to medicine, or it may be seemingly unrelated, as physics is to college administration. A physicist may become a college president; if so, he is likely to take his administrative style from physics. A person's competence has its home in his profession; his philosophic depth is based in his discipline. In a survey some years ago, more heads of large corporations were found to have had baccalaureates in English than in any other field, and one would suspect that this condition still prevails. Recently, for the first time, a survey of upper managers showed a majority to have graduate work in management. But this finding hardly refutes my argument: graduate work is properly professional; undergraduate work is not.

What I have briefly outlined is the theory of a liberal education. Perhaps few educators would express it in this way, but most, I believe, would accept the general notion as the ideal behind college education in our nation. All too often the ideal is compromised by timidity, stemming from a fear of impracticality. We are all so shot through with behaviorism that we automatically fall into the position of preconceiving what students should learn or what they should be and accordingly setting about modifying behavior to accomplish those aims. We are misled by suppositions of short-range efficiency and cannot abandon our students to the fullness and freedom of learning. It is difficult for many of us to believe that it is precisely the non-utilitarian commitment that endows liberal education with its transforming power. The experience of that power is not the privilege of an intellectual elite but the right of every person. All are able to participate in it. By means of this potent alchemy education benefits society, although it accomplishes its purpose by changing individuals, one by one, as it inducts them into the learning process.

For an institution to persist in offering a liberal education, it must be granted a great deal of freedom—indeed, it must be protected and nurtured. I have spoken of the timidity of educators in diminishing the range of study, but perhaps, instead of timidity, their attitude should be considered caution. The sponsoring body of a university rarely understands the true function of education for society and, operating on its own wisdom, seeks to improve the educational process by limiting the authority of educators. The state as sponsor quite naturally falls into this limiting position. Its artificial separation of education from religion while at the same time tying education to the state is a very clear and present danger to society. We need perhaps to remember that only in our time, only after World War II, has the government been the dominant sponsor of higher education in this country. And only in this time has the attempt been made to provide a totally secular school system. Whether or not a society can long endure without inculcating the idea of the sacred is a very fair question, as the anthropologist Mircea Eliade has pointed out. And I can add my warning that presently observable portents are not promising.

The state introduces its limitations through funding procedures and other devices that effectively bring education into the political realm; and, where limitations are prevented by law, licensing prevails, extending dangerously into the private sector. One can certainly not say that private education is free of limitations. Its governing boards are as much affected as those of state schools by the late nineteenth-century concept of efficiency and its contemporary counterpart, the widely misunderstood principle of productivity. They are many times far more reluctant even than state schools to leave special interests to the vagaries of inquiry. Nonetheless, for all the proprietary air of their sponsors, independent colleges have more freedom, and freedom of a more fundamental sort, than politically controlled institutions.

I would not wish to be misunderstood on this point. State-sponsored education has been of tremendous benefit to society. Public higher education by its nature must have shorter-range, more immediate goals than those of independent education; practicality plays a larger role in its total program. Since the support of tax money releases the several state universities from the financial constraints imposed either by free enterprise or by philanthropy, the development of each school must be controlled by a state-wide planning board. Still, any one school must have the freedom to express a character, a seeming independence, if it is to fill its role in society. The regional state university should be an expression of its local community, should hold its pieties, so to speak, and in a sense universalize them. A city needs to protect its state schools from the regime, from standardization and the natural tendency to reduce public education to the least common denominator.

Similarly, community colleges should not be restricted to purely practical matters. They, too, are part of the myth-making process that once went on chiefly in the home but now is relegated to schools, a mythopoiesis that reanimates the virtues and invigorates spiritual forces within the community. These locally supported colleges have the task of liberal education for the benefit of society and can fulfill their task if they are allowed to approach their work boldly. Too often they are made to feel that they must offer their courses under the subterfuge of teaching people to read, write, and figure in order to hold a job. The social significance of liberal education—whatever its specific content—lies in its ability to preserve the dignity of the individual: to conceive of him as a whole person, capable finally of making moral judgments.

It is true, however, that state- or community-controlled schools look to independent colleges for the model of education. For this reason, in the difficult times that lie ahead, the importance of private schools' maintaining the liberal attitude as I have characterized it cannot be overestimated.

How we come through the approaching troubled times will depend largely on the strength and wisdom of the generation now being readied for leadership. Proper concern for their formation is the fearful responsibility of educational institutions and, indeed, the shared burden of all those who shape the future.

10

College Education and Leadership

WHAT IS THIS BUSINESS OF LEADERSHIP? According to a classic theory concerning the levels of command, one man tends to command eight others, and each of these eight others. The tree-shaped levels therefore look like this:

```
            1                  0
            8                  1
          6   4                2     0.02%
         5  1  2               3
        4  0  9  6             4
       3  2  7  6  8           5
      2  6  2  1  4  4         6     1%
     2  0  9  7  1  5  2       7
    1  6  7  7  7  2  1  6     8     9%
   1  3  4  2  1  7  7  2  8   9     90%
```

Everyone in America of college age and up is in the tree. There are only nine levels altogether. Where does each of us stand? The tree is symbolic, descriptive of a strict authoritarian system. Where would the poets fit—the artists—the revolutionists? But I propose that the gradations on any system of evaluation probably run about the same. Let me call them "levels of significance," and we can interpret them however we will.

We should notice that 90% of all people are in the bottom

layer, 9% are in the next one up. We need to remember that about 20% of the present generation will earn a college degree; fewer than half of these will advance as high as level eight. The next two levels up—six and seven—contain 1% of the population. These are the people who maintain society, who accept responsibility and make operating decisions. Industry calls this level middle management. To call it "middle significance" would be to underplay it because it involves real qualities of leadership—only one in a hundred attain it. Eight to ten years will pass after the college graduate leaves school before he is "elected," so to say, to this level.

But what about those upper five levels? What about that 0.02% of the population that industry would call Top Management or we would call highly significant—as critics, philosophers, scientists, businessmen, or whatever these persons might be? In the nation maybe two thousand persons each year reach level five. Are we schooling our students for these posts—positions or honors or whatever one calls them—that they will attain thirty or forty years after they graduate? A realization of this time gap between schooling and position makes the scheme of education pursued in a university much more meaningful. Obviously what must be done is to plant the seeds which, once rooted, will grow over a long period of time. What a curriculum should do is to transform the person rather than train him. We could no more teach a person all he needs to know to reach the top than we could build a skyscraper to the moon. If we are to send a person to the moon we can only start him in the right direction and turn him loose. But further, the persons who reach the rarefied levels of upper significance are different in kind from those who do not. They were not born different; *somewhere along the way they have been transformed.* I will not say that native intelligence is not of some consequence; but I do say it is not controlling and that, in any sense, most college students are above the threshold of inheritance and into the region of will. The shape college gives their lives now and the limitations they accept are matters of choice.

What are the choices and how does the will operate in driving a person toward leadership? Can one, by sheer grit and determination, penetrate through to the upper levels? I do not doubt that a person can set goals and develop personality and Dale-Carnegie it through to level seven—into middle management. That is no mean accomplishment, even admirable in the untransformed person. But the qualities of leadership are far more complex, the process of transformation far more subtle than can be accomplished by any direct attack.

There are two countervailing movements in the process of transformation to significance. The first I would label *the realization of the self.* The significant person is unique and is conscious of his uniqueness. He has a job to do that has never been done before. He takes on a task because he knows that in the scheme of things he is the one who is supposed to do it. He knows that in the major drama of his life he is the hero. Admitting this, how does a person obtain this self-realization? What studies does he make, what exercises does he do?

The variety is infinite, ranging through physical awareness to spiritual ecstasy. Playing football, or to a somewhat lesser degree taking part in any sport, provides great opportunity for the unification of body and mind. So does dancing. A person can attain a sense of being wholly himself through play, through becoming alert to the elaborate sensory and communication system within him which allows him to respond as a unit to phenomena and to exercise some control in the responses. He discovers his interface with the outside world and recognizes the realm of his withinness. What I am saying is that play is not a trivial thing, not something to be discarded early in life. It is one of the avenues to self-realization.

But there are many others. The first two years of a college curriculum should be largely devoted to accomplishing this realization of the self. The development of the tools of communication—primarily writing—into highly individualized instruments of expression, fully as unique to the person as his fingerprints, is essential to this accomplishment. There are other tools and skills that become unified in the person; but, more than the acquisition of skills, the first two years of college are intended to place the individual in the environment of history, to make him aware again of the interface that delimits him and the necessity to communicate across it. The curriculum in these two years is expected to provide occasions of triumph. Recently, a bright student whom I know, after deciding to drop a computer course, said with engaging frankness, "It's damaging my ego." He may have been right to drop it at his stage of development; or the fact that he was that much aware of himself may indicate a readiness for the next stage of development.

And there is another stage of development. Not only must the person of significance go through a realization of the self as a unit, a discovery of the ego, but he must also experience a *submergence of the self*, a loss of ego. This stage is more difficult; fewer people accomplish it. But it is essential to greatness. This stage should dominate the last two years of college. These are the years of submission to a discipline. The transition from an ambition for mastery to a willingness— even a desire—for submission is the great step toward significance. I suppose one could call it "from lust to love," and certainly it is in the guise of love that a discipline comes to a person. One chooses a major course of study and comes in time to submit to its discipline. Some people never do submit but go on thinking of a major as an accomplishment, a trophy to hang on their belts, seeking to collect several as a display of their many talents. Such people are still in stage one, still in the development of the ego, and for them we realize that any growth toward leadership has not yet begun.

How does one recognize this transition? I have said that the discipline comes in the guise of love. There is a glory that shines around it. There is a joy in it and, as in love, a great deal of agony. It is something for which one is willing like Ferdinand to hew wood and draw water. This is not a sentimental notion I am presenting; it really does occur. It ought to occur about the middle of one's junior year. And sometimes it happens in the last year of undergraduate work. But one is fortunate if it happens at all. I recently heard a graduating senior remark, "I may have to make my living in a filling station, but my life will be in physics."

The choice of a discipline is tremendously important. It is not, however, the disciplines which concern me here so much as the act of submission. My characterization of the first two years as the realization of the self and the second two as the submergence of the self is by no means strict. Just as the acts of realization go on throughout life, the acts of submission begin early. One understands a poem or a work of art only through an act of submission, through taking in and being taken in by the thing in all its wholeness. The same is true of philosophic or mathematical ideas, although the process is more difficult when the rational element seems to dominate. One discovers a habit of soul that seeks not to master but to submit to all experience, to know it for what it is and to become part of it.

These two oppositely directed motions, realization and submergence, go on simultaneously in a person, forming a kind of plasma of being. A person of a religious bent, incidentally, has an advantage in awareness of this duality because he knows both his responsibility and his unworthiness—knows that he must strive for salvation and yet be saved by grace. The two must come together. Perhaps we can understand Milton a little better when he says "Fame is the spur that the pure spirit doth raise/That last infirmity of noble minds." There is that last submergence of the self, that last submission to grace that is still to be accomplished.

And certainly grace will come to us. There is a grace of office adequate for every task we are called to do. In the amazing generosity under which we live, grace awaits us, not to grasp by desire but to submit to by will. It is only by such receptivity that a person can take his place as a leader.

SCIENCE, TECHNOLOGY, AND SOCIETY

11

The Technological Imagination

THE NEW SOCIETY now well underway is technological rather than industrial. Technology has so increased productivity that industry is no longer the chief employer in the American economy, no longer the model for all aspects of society. The models that will characterize the new society are not yet apparent: they will emerge not as technology but because of it, given freedom to take on lineaments more nearly expressive of society's hopes and aspirations. Technology empowers aspirations. But, we might go on to ask, what is new about technology? It has been around for a long time, probably from the very beginning of human history. It is the second most important gift of Prometheus to the human race—the first being "blind hopes" that enabled mortals to focus less on their inevitable death than on how they would use their lives.

In Aeschylus' account of the story, as we remember, only Prometheus among the gods opposed Zeus' plan to destroy the human race. Prometheus saved mankind from extinction and, further, from the darkness of ignorance. "I gave him mind, the use of intellect," he declares in his account of the origins of consciousness, ending, "Wherefore in one short word learn everything: Prometheus taught *all* arts to human kind." *Techné* is the word he uses, technique, as we call it, the art of making things: the *how* of doing anything well, according to its purpose. For this generosity to humankind and his subsequent refusal to repent, Prometheus is hurled into blackest Tartarus, where Zeus' "winged vulture hound" will daily tear at his liver.

Techné is a godlike quality, possessed on Olympus most supremely by the divine blacksmith Hephaestus. Yet it was perceived by Prometheus to be necessary to the very nature of mankind. We ourselves rather take it for granted, confidently saying *man the toolmaker*, supposing by such a designation that we differentiate ourselves from every other creature. Perhaps one ought not be so certain of this accolade. In an age when pigeons can learn to push a button to obtain a grain of corn from a machine and rats can be trained to turn a spigot, it is hard not to think that animals may be just biding their time before taking over, waiting until human beings have perfected technology to a point worth using. At any rate, it is technology—in a sense an afterthought for man, not part of his original endowment, as this early myth would have it—that enables the human race to be specifically human.

Technology, too, motivates the second of the mythic heroes whose struggles for knowledge illumine the scientific quest. Marlowe's Dr. Faustus, in his desire to surmount the limitations of the mortal mind, turns to magic, seeking absolute control over time and space. He summons up a familiar spirit, Mephistophilis, whose seeming ability to make all things possible suggests an impersonal source of energy, much like electricity. For twenty-four years he serves at Faustus' command, conveying to the magician virtually unlimited power, which Faustus trivializes to satisfy curiosity and appetite. If Marlowe's drama is a governing myth for modernity, as I believe we could maintain it is, then its portrait of the human psyche should be sobering to us, since it is far less grand than that implied in dramas of previous epochs. In *Faustus* the dominant motives are individual gratification and inventiveness, rather than the grand old sins—pride, ambition, aspiration—of the ancient world. In Marlowe's version, Faustus is carried down to hell as punishment for his quest for forbidden knowledge. In Goethe's reexamination of the myth two and a half centuries later, Faust changes the biblical "In the beginning was the word" to "In the beginning was the deed." Action, accomplishment: these are the important goals for the Faustian—that is, the modern—mind. At the end, in Goethe's version, Faust is assumed into heaven, after conquering the entire world with his technology and humanitarian purpose. Though he harms a great many people, Goethe would have him saved by his soaring imagination and by something in the universe—the *ewig weibliche*, the eternal feminine—that loves and pities. The moral evaluations in the two versions of the Faust drama are different, but the interpretation of Faust is the same: he has found a way to *do* things with knowledge, not merely to know.

In both these myths depicting the quest for knowledge—the Faustian and the Promethean—the kind of knowledge gained is technological. Its purpose in both stories is to improve man's material lot, either individually or socially. One might begin a definition of technology with this grand desire for the betterment of men, noting the necessity of ingenious apparatus to accomplish this end. There seems to be in technology an implicit aspiration to spread its benefits to all. Its early stages require specially trained operators, an initiate, to mediate the benefits; but as any single aspect of the process defines itself, its arcane nature is transferred to the apparatus. Anyone can make use of it. In such a way equality is fostered —but at the cost of some depersonalization in work accomplished. Hence its effect is double. And throughout history, this same duplicity has accompanied its influence. Praise and blame are equally easily associated with it. Prometheus and Faust are in some sense admirable, in another blameworthy. Like the dog Lion who bays the great bear in Faulkner's

Go Down, Moses, technology can be viewed paradoxically; and hence the reflections of Isaac McCaslin could perhaps apply to all of us in our attitude to the technological age now upon us:

> So he should have hated and feared Lion. Yet he did not. It seemed to him that there was a fatality in it. It seemed to him that something, he didn't know what, was beginning, had already begun. It was like the last act on a set stage. It was the beginning of the end of something, he didn't know what except that he would not grieve. He would be humble and proud that he had been found worthy to be a part of it too or even just to see it too.

The new order which Isaac knows will destroy both the bear and the old order is a technological *age*, not simply technology as a supplement to or an improvement upon the ordinary human way of doing things. As the dominant economic mode, it represents a new era for human culture, one that—still following Faulkner's underlying typology—is inevitable in the course of Christianity. As such it brings not peace but a sword, requiring choice. It can be seen as the Promethean hope—the way in which humanity increasingly raises itself and its culture from a brutish state; or, in contrast, as the Faustian way, which, by substituting raw power for a human order, separates people from community and from their own nature.

In the fictive working of *poiesis*, technology fares poorly. The entire course of the novelistic tradition seems to condemn it. Yet lurking in the lines of even the most dour accounts of mankind's ingenuity are prophetic implications, an unwilling eschatology of hope. Much of that hope lies in an increase in human knowledge, a great part of which is an unfolding of understanding through the sciences, from which technology derives.

A few years ago an essay of mine drew the conventional distinction between "pure" science and its offshoots;

> Pure Science is an effort devoted to the extension of fundamental knowledge. Applied Science takes the discoveries of pure science and

makes them useful for society. Technology builds, operates, and maintains the apparatus applied science develops. Technology thus stands in service to applied science.

These three levels of science suggest a hierarchy of respectability that in our present context, however, may not be justified. It is usually accepted that pure science is one of the liberal arts and that applied science is not. But I suspect the crucified Prometheus looks at such a division with a liver-jaundiced eye. "I taught man all the arts," he declares in his own self-defense; and, as he makes clear, underlying and permeating the useful arts is the act of understanding. Before they could master skills and crafts, men had eyes but saw not, ears, but heard not. They had to be able to do before they could know. In depicting the making and doing, the imaginative acts that lead to society, the Prometheus story is less about forbidden knowledge than about the origins of human culture.

Yet the familiar defining characteristic of liberal learning is its direction toward knowledge for its own sake and not for use. Cardinal Newman made that point as Aristotle had made it many centuries before. Certainly science, in its essence, is directed toward knowledge and not toward products. Its fundamental action is the expansion of knowledge for its own sake. It *is* a liberal art. Few disciples of any sect surpass in ardor and self-forgetfulness the scientist in pursuit of knowledge; monks of the secular world, we might call them, busy at their devotions. But we know, too, that once the understanding of a phenomenon becomes widespread, it is quickly turned toward use. Joy in knowledge for its own sake and joy in putting knowledge to use are not greatly separated in any actual creative endeavor. Perhaps, then, even the theoretical scientist cannot be entirely unaware of the practical applications of his work. To be innocent of the consequences of one's actions is a definition of madness.

In any analysis of the technological age now before us, we must recognize that human beings cannot effectively separate thought and action—that, in fact such an attempt may effect a dangerous split in our consciousness. Techniques cannot without danger be separated from content; skills cannot be learned without thought and judgment. My perspective in these remarks, however, is cultural, not educational: that is, I am concerned with analyzing the new stage of culture in which we find ourselves and assessing the roles that science and technology have played in producing it.

Culture refers to more than the fine arts and intellectual niceties; it implies the whole manner in which society operates, in forms partly created, partly given—its work, food, customs. A culture is elevated by the infusion of science; its intellectual inquiry is made more precise and elegant by scientific thought; its economy is made more affluent as the findings of science are made useful. As a culture is heightened, the ability of its members to seek further knowledge is enhanced. It is an exponentially increasing process. What Zeus feared—that man would come to think like the gods—seems ever nearer. Perhaps Zeus was right in punishing Prometheus. Yet, as the Titan prophetically saw, it is man's destiny to know.

The process by which pure scientific knowledge filters down to the practical plane is hierarchical, with levels that were fairly well separated in former years. New knowledge about the world is discovered by scientists and made practical by engineers. But in recent times, the distinction has become less clear-cut. An interim group has arisen—applied scientists —who themselves seek knowledge directly for use. This development provides power for the current of immense gains in technology that has brought us into the technological age.

To classify the present age as technological is to recognize a shift in the sensibility of people toward what they are doing. The age preceding ours was industrial, institutionalized for the manufacture of products—typically durable goods such as automobiles, refrigerators, and air conditioners, together with the immense factory machinery needed to produce them. The factory dominated our minds; *production* was the mark of the industrial era.

In a technological age, in contrast to industrialism, it is the *use* of apparatus, not its production, that stands as symbolic of the time. What is important is not the display of something, but its function. The automobile, a product of industrialism, remains with the new order as a status symbol, an object to be displayed. It is not important that it can *travel* a hundred miles an hour but that it look like it can. On the other hand, the personal computer—an instrument of technology—remains in the back room; its programs, what it can do, are its source of satisfaction. The software, so to say, is its symbol. And single-purpose micro-computers are everywhere; we use them without thought. They are, as Marshall McLuhan predicted, extensions of our central nervous system. At the time when he made that statement, it seemed negative: people would be plugged into a huge device, providing a systematized group experience—a frightening picture of a beehive society. Instead, as it has turned out, the micro-computers are in effect plugged into us, dedicated to do a task at our bidding. We and not they are the masters; they are the slaves. Technology thus goes underground, out of our awareness. Plastics, the tip given to Dustin Hoffman in *The Graduate*, did indeed become our introduction to high-technology and since then has gone on to make itself into an effectively invisible substructure of our society. The invidious term "plastic people" has fallen away because of its manifest inappropriateness: plastic, in many forms, has shown itself to be a supple and accommodating medium, more able than natural material to follow the curvings of imagination.

When I say technology has gone underground, exceptions to my statement can be found in medical technology, which in retaining its high visibility, its hierarchical structure, and its arcane mode of operation, functions according to the past age of mechanism. Medicine is still something done *to* us, not by us. It is highly institutionalized, so that people must go to medical centers and seek aid, interrupting the normal course of their lives, rather than having health as an integrated element of their ordinary projects. Medicine is a remnant of the age of enlightenment, when professionals and specialists carefully marked off the territory they were bound to protect. That situation will shortly change.

For the most part, our cultural imaginations have absorbed technology. The metaphors by which we communicate and with which we think comprehend the new age on the level at which it is shared generally by the community. Subtly our language shifts to reflect a new intent: automation was an industrial threat; computerization is a technological aid. Blind hope, perhaps, but such a shift in language is a remarkably human accommodation to the gift of techné.

Imagination is the instrument through which new scientific information enters the world. This is that Promethean fire that generated all the arts—a gift from the abode of the gods, an opening into a realm beyond the reservoirs of knowledge, beyond the range of reason. If used merely as inventiveness reined in by self-interest, as the Faustian myth would have it, the technological imagination returns the tawdry gifts deserved. But if applied in self-forgetfulness, in simple acceptance of what is to come and acknowledgement of the good in the work to be done, the technological imagination looks forward to a reconciliation between Zeus and Prometheus, opening its fires of prophecy and rewarding mankind with intuitions of hope.

How do these intuitions reach our consciousness? In images, past epochs have testified. The image is a visual thing. But it is no great extension to generalize and by *visual* to understand *sensory*, for all of our senses take in patterns that carry meaning. Sight, sound, touch, taste, and smell all evince identity that we can call image. *Tabula rasa* to the contrary, I suspect certain images are present in the imagination as archetypes. In walking the great plains of the West, one can hear a cicada or a dry rustle that possibly could be a rattlesnake, but when one actually hears that ominous warning, identification is unmistakable. It is already known and immediately matched to the signal. All animals know it, and fear is its companion. But archetypes aside, however they got there images populate the memory and, called up into the imagination, are the substance, we might say, for rumination, contemplation, and thought.

Is visualization a necessary element? Must there be a picture image or geometric construct in the mind in order to think with the imagination? For example, can we think about the solar system with planets revolving about the sun, each in its own orbit, without a mental picture? Such an image is a construct; no one has ever seen it; it must be put together from measurements. It seems real and is useful. But is it necessary? Henri Poincaré, the French mathematician, insisted that most of his colleagues thought geometrically, in pictures; but there are those rare minds, he admitted, who seemingly go directly to analytics and deny visualization. Imageless images would seem to be strange entities, but for such minds the process of thought appears to form an intellectual pattern neither visual nor verbal—the diffuse cloud of knowing coalescing into numbers, not figures.

The most famous controversy on visualization in physics concerned the atom, the photon, and the indeterminacy principle, with Niels Bohr, Max Planck, and Albert Einstein on one side and Werner Heisenberg on the other. Physics from its beginnings with early Greek astronomy has been a process of model building, of visualizing an event in an imaginary space. It has kept that character even up through the present cosmogony. Lord Rutherford visualized the invisible atom as a pudding of positive charge with negative electrons imbedded like raisins. But when he fired alpha particles from radium at a gold foil, these positive particles bounced off as if they had struck a hard positive nucleus at the center of a gold atom with mostly empty space around. The electrons then would be like planets traversing their orbits about the sun in a miniature Copernican universe. Bohr, about 1913, adapted that model with some judicious and startling changes and produced the picture of the single-electron hydrogen atom that most of us retain to this day, an electron circling a proton in one of a set of allowed orbits. The figure became the rationale of calculations.

All of this was quite visual and reasonably causal, in keeping with the long tradition of physical theory from Galileo on. There were some difficulties: the electron did not radiate as a circling charge should according to electro-magnetic theory; the electron jumped from orbit to orbit seemingly without passing through the space between, thus violating the principle of continuity of position; and when it jumped it emitted a photon carrying off the energy difference of the orbits. Some *ad hoc* postulates were required to repair these seeming ruptures in classical theory, but still Bohr's construction of the atom (an electron circling a proton) gave a fairly satisfying visual model.

Unfortunately, though the model of the atom as a miniature solar system worked well for hydrogen, it failed to yield right answers for helium or any of the other multi-electron atoms, no matter how ingeniously it was employed. Heisenberg therefore chose to disregard entirely the concept of a model and work with a strictly mathematical matrix representation of "virtual oscillators." When he introduced Planck's constant into the matrix, suddenly things fell into place: in one night of feverish work he produced quantum mechanics. "I seemed to be looking into a strange new world," he said, inspired by its beauty. Nonetheless, despite his metaphor, in his scheme there were no visual models, no geometric arrangements that could be analyzed for values. It

was all mathematics, yielding not precise quantities but prob-
abilistic answers. Heisenberg became convinced that models
were a hindrance to thought in physical theory and cam-
paigned vigorously for his point of view—a cause, incidentally, that the French phenomenologist Gaston Bachelard
took up, making it the basis for his total separation of poetry
and science, though he published in both literary criticism
and philosophy of science. "I felt duty bound," says Bachelard, "to exorcise the images which claimed to engender and
maintain concepts in a scientific culture."

But the model had long been too fruitful a device to be cast
aside easily. Not many months after Heisenberg formulated
his unvisualizable quantum mechanics, which treated the
photon in effect as a particle, Erwin Schrödinger developed
his wave mechanics, treating the photon as a wave that in a
sense could be visualized. The model-building cause-relators
—Bohr, Einstein, and others—lined up behind wave
mechanics so that it seemed as if the old particle/wave battle
of Newton/Huygens would be on again. But a year later
Schrödinger showed that the two different-appearing theories
were really the same. The photon is one entity with dual
characteristics, wave and particle, visualizable or not as one
chooses.

In a sense Heisenberg lost his battle against the model, but
at least he showed that it was a voluntary, not a necessary,
concept. We do not have to visualize in order to imagine.
Most often, however, we do form images in our minds during
the imaginative process, calling up actual pictures or diagrams
according to our bent.

That duality of possibilities should give us some clue concerning the workings of the scientific imagination. Various
accounts of how the great discoveries have come about,
Heisenberg's among them, should provide another. Invariably these accounts indicate a long period of rigorous
thought along conventional lines, with the mind finally

exhausted, in a state of temporary failure, one could say. At such a time the will is relaxed so that it does not intervene; it allows phantasms to appear from memory or archetype (from what Yeats has named the two great storehouses: the Great Memory and the Great Mind), watching idly the quasi-scenarios they form. At rare times, some concatenation reshapes itself and completes its form through a process that obviously is not random. Nor is it produced by ingenuity: the will is still pliant, but recognition is alert. The readiness is all, apparently. Though never seen before, a certain presentation is recognized as authentic and the recognition verified by an accompanying joy. Then the will awakes and the hard work begins, the mathematical work that lends rigor and communicability to the insight. This sequence, I think, marks the action of the imagination—an admission, a seemingly free association, a recognition. In the process, I should point out, the fullness of the insight is stripped down to the abstraction of consistency. True, the calculations that ensue will be in agreement with the model now in the mind, but the model presented to the world, such as Bohr's atom, has already been reshaped by thought. It is the residue of insight, not the thing itself. The radiant form is not present. The model does not have the full authenticity of revelation, and in fine the mathematical development carries more authority than the model.

It seems clear that Heisenberg's work (without the model) was as much a product of imagination as was Schrödinger's (with the model). But for Heisenberg the imagination operated in a different realm from the spatio-temporal and geometric. Quite possibly it was in a mythopoetic mode. At any rate, it was forerunner of the new age, a turn away from Renaissance figuralism and Romantic image. The culture that we are now partially constructing, partially submitting to, is, like the Middle Ages, an age of forms rather than images.

Obviously the imagination I have been describing is that of an artist, the extraordinary scientist of whom Thomas Kuhn speaks, one who sees and makes; and I suspect that the process is not greatly different for poet and physicist. Perhaps the characteristic that distinguishes great minds from others is not brilliance nor hard work but acceptance—acceptance of failure, we might say, so that the will relaxes and the mind walks among presences, be they archetypes or angels, that come visiting out of the plenitude of reality. Truth, it seems, is not an argument but a presence.

The imagination is available to all, not simply to geniuses. But when we drop down a level to the ordinary scientist, the normal scientist, Kuhn calls him, we find in his acceptance of images an admission requirement not so exclusive, an association level not so free, a recognition criterion not so fundamental. What floats in the imagination of the ordinary scientist is not archetypes but models, things that already exist in the conscious minds of other men. The desire that leads an ordinary investigator to the recognition of pertinent patterns and forms is directed toward perfecting an already existent paradigm guiding the investigation. That is no mean goal. It is a noble mind that seeks knowledge, and if fame is the spur for the ordinary scientist it is a modest and self-effacing sort of fame.

The concept of paradigm deserves some comment. It is Kuhn's term for a dominant world view or an originary model in a particular activity that governs way of thinking. It is initiated by an insight of an extraordinary mind but is not, in itself, wholly contained in that artist's particular work. Science is a communal affair and hence the paradigm is built by many minds and hands. The individual work disappears from the body of science, to be laid to rest in history or psychology. That dismissive action rather troubles Kuhn the historian but is fully in accord with what I call the residual nature of science. Science discards its artifacts while retaining their knowledge.

All this has to do with pure science. What about applied science? Actually, in their workings, normal science and applied science do not greatly differ. Both are devoted to problem solving. The imagination of both is goal-dominated. (I am not speaking of extraordinary science.) All scientific experiment, even in the purest of scientific adventures, is purposeful. Research is never simply puttering about to see what happens; it is always designed to answer some question; and whatever unexpected or serendipitous events may be observed in the pursuit must be set aside for later decisions until, to use medical imagery, after the operation is finished, even though the patient may have died on the table. When laboratory people say "Let's see what happens," the answer that ought to be given by the research director is always, "No, let's *imagine* what will happen." Only then can we judge whether or not the apparatus we have and our scheme for using it will produce meaningful information. And in the imagination a goal is set.

In this aspect of its functioning, the imagination is controlled, manipulated, restricted; it is an image-processor, equally useful in pure or applied science, in engineering or the writing of poetry. Frequently the imagined experiment is transferred to a computer to play theme and variation to its end. To what degree the computer inhibits imagination or releases it remains a fair question, but it has eliminated an enormous amount of useless fiddling around. As an aid to thought, it takes the patterns of the old order and extends them in scope far beyond what could ordinarily be done with them. In this sense, the computer bridges the gap between the old and the new.

But there *is* a difference between pure and applied science. The distinction between the two, we were saying, lies in the imagination's being directed toward *knowing*, for the pure scientist, toward *using* for the applied scientist. And along this thin line we separate the liberal from the useful. Here, too, in its restricted and popular sense, begins technology.

Despite its utilitarian bent, applied science is difficult to banish completely from the hallowed laboratories of selfless interest. Too many important discoveries, not just techniques, have had their origin in commercial enterprises for us to ignore their contributions. Even paradigms have been born in such delivery rooms. Knowledge of the solid state is more than a stepchild of industry, and the transistor was conceived in the patient womb of good gray Ma Bell. An enlightened policy toward thinkers has caused industrialists to simulate academia—indeed go it better—in providing facilities, time, and even scope in order that scientists in their employ may be productive. Yet in the end, in these circumstances, profit must prevail; things must be usable. And success for the industrial scientist must not be too infrequent.

Probably the most active field of high-tech development at present is biotechnology. Just a few years ago recombinant dna, gene-splicing, cloning, and such techniques were firmly located in pure science. Now some hundred and fifty small companies are busy commercializing this field. The journal *Science* reports on one of them: "in its creation of new major products, Genentech has a record that no other pharmaceutical company has matched in recent years. In part this success is due to the fact that Genentech was early in applying recombinant DNA to create new products. In part success has arisen from its judicious choice of projects to tackle." Judicious choice—that is, the ability to envision the end point, the goal, of imagination—is something that is likely to have a good market, a practical manufacturing process, and a short period before production. When such concerns entirely govern recognition, however, the imagination can easily becomes the instrument of ingenuity rather than insight, of fancy rather than imagination.

Nothing is inherently wrong in this state of affairs. It is disturbing, perhaps, but not wrong. The system is supposed to work in this way. What science discovers and develops to the point of understanding is taken over by technology, rendered practical, and made subject to the rigors of free enterprise. Science moves serenely on to the next mystery.

In setting up *use* as the criterion for recognition in the technological imagination, I have indicated a resultant economic pattern demanding a profitable product. Almost unwittingly I thus have tied the technological age back to the preceding industrial age. But my intention is not to diminish its radical distinctness. A new medium of any sort always establishes itself by imitating the old, rides on its back, profits by doing some of the same things better. But even in its early stages, technology does more than facilitate industry. The word-processor improves on the typewriter so that a typist can produce perfect letters more efficiently; but it ends by eliminating the typist. The male dictator and the female secretary are in the process of disappearing as much because of technology as because of a triumphalist feminist movement. Technology seeks to leap process. The personal computer becomes an extension of the writer, the thinker, the decision-maker. On a larger scale, the computer begins by facilitating an industrial organization and ends by dissipating it. Similarly, the new biotechnology will begin by giving doctors new tools and new medicines and end, through preventive medicine and other methods of curing, by changing the concept of the physician.

The new technology is not electronics, not solid state, not wrinkle-proof fabrics with teflon coating, not recombinant dna, gene-splicing, artificial insulin. It is imagination turned toward use, toward ends beyond foreseeable ends. The apparatus is merely a black box, available to the most innocent of users. We approach simplicity by complex means. Technology urges us toward simplicity—a simpler economy, a simpler market place, a simpler life. We need not indulge in prophetic vision to sense this movement nor project a paradise. It is still a fallen world in which we dwell. But it is not quite so frightening or so ugly as it once seemed. Technologism is a step better than industrialism. Science has strange children, but not all are monsters.

But now we might return for a few minutes to that thin line where technology begins, that region above the line where science is the wellspring for technology, where imagination is directed toward knowledge. The degree of profundity issuing from imagination, I have indicated, is in relation to the degree by which the will can be relaxed, can be released from reason, from desire, from taste or fitness or manners or whatever purpose governs the mind. Failure triggers a release, a failure of thought in its exhaustion, so that reason subsides; a failure of desire to satisfy, of taste to please. In defeat accepted is release. Conservation laws are set aside. The absurd has its fleeting moments. On the stage of the imagination archetypes or angels appear.

It is this state of reverie that Bachelard calls the surrational, just outside rationality; and, to relate it to our topic, we might call it more generally the supracultural, for what is brought back from that realm across the border must have meaning in the current culture. What is retrieved comes back at the disposition of the retriever as visual, conceptual, or emotive—as form, line, rhythm, proposition, or other manifestation of an insight into the mythic structure of a society. Already the original insight has suffered one abstraction in the retrieval process and now an additional one is imposed as the passions, as I would put it, take over. Reverie turns to desire, encompassing, possessing, making what is strange and lovely into a familiar presence within the discipline. The sciences alter their criteria for admission in order to include the new bride. Physics must follow reason, but a reason that has been expanded to accommodate the new material. Reason conforms itself to truth, not the reverse. The other sciences—chemistry, biology—are not so strictly reasonable,

having for their abstractions incomplete geometric constructions that illustrate rather than argue logically. But these
figures serve well, nonetheless. From them rivulets trickle
down across the thin border into technology. "There is a
forest of models," says the French thinker Michel Serres, "of
which reason is only one. Sometimes a person is so close to
his model he cannot see the forest." It is this sense of a larger
terrain—a shadowy, mysterious forest which one enters and
out of which one may cut many paths—that sustains the
vitality of any kind of learning. Other disciplines as well as
the sciences have similar avenues out of the supracultural
whereby truth is infused into culture. In this manner a society
accumulates its practical *speculum mentis*, its map of the mundane mind.

* * *

In the end, as I suppose I have been saying all along, the
Promethean fire is imagination, not simply skills or reason;
and imagination is the power from a divine source whereby
matter is permeated with spirit. To be sure, this divine fire
casts its shadow—an obscurity all the more dark *because* of
the light. Sometimes when we peer into this blackness, we
become convinced that it, not the light, is the reality; and in
contrast with this dire vision, even the non-knowing of the
savage state before Prometheus' gift seems preferable. There is
a darkness shadowing technology; there *are* dark times coming. The transition from one major epoch to another is not to
be accomplished handily. But our response to all the ensuing
problems must not be to turn against the light—for it is by
means of the poetic and technological illumination that
human life has been lifted from its enslavement to matter and
directed toward the liberty for which it seems destined.

12

The New Technology and the Polis

TECHNOLOGY AND CIVILIZATION are inextricably intertwined: one simply does not exist without the other. The advances of civilization are for the most part the advances of technology. By giving larger scope to human action, these innovations provide increased largesse for culture, greater space and material for art and thought. Eventually any technology becomes so thoroughly absorbed in a civilization as to be invisible, sustaining and supporting without fanfare all the comings and goings of life. Awareness of an established technology becomes, given sufficient time, unconscious and intuitive, submerged beneath habitual actions. But any new technology that initiates a shift in a civilization is always highly visible and always threatening.

Innovations in technology can generally be categorized as those that provide increases in materials, power, transportation, and information. The stages of a society may be identified by the innovations in any one of these classes: in the first, materials, we ordinarily make the familiar division into Stone, Bronze, Iron, Steel, and Plastic Ages. In a similar way we can think of the sources of power, from wood, coal, oil, and now nuclear energy. Likewise, the avenues of transportation represent distinct steps in the advance of civilization—rivers, seas, highways, railroads, airways, and outer space. So too the methods of recording, disseminating, or manipulating information, from early symbols to writing, printing, radio-broadcasting, television, and information-processing by computers.

But before we get into a story of technology in our day we should perhaps examine the ground from which it springs. Technology is without doubt the outgrowth of science, but not in the way one would easily suppose—that is, that a scientific discovery conceived in disinterested purity becomes exploited by economic and materialistic motives. In point of fact, science springs as much from technology as technology from science. In my own experience, an interest in the structure of water in the "purest," most disinterested sense came from an assignment to change brackish to potable water. And if we go back to Galileo's times and before, we find that the interest in rockets, projectiles, and falling bodies was motivated by military needs. Practical demand can, and frequently does, instigate a new direction in science.

But it is not so much the pragmatic relationship with society that I would consider the progenitor of science as it is the myth that is current in a culture. Science is the dramatic exploration of a myth, and in this respect it shares with religion a quite fundamental responsibility for the integrity of a people's belief. Myths have to do with how things come about —creation, the discovery of fire, the founding of cities. Inherent in the how is the why—the metaphysical foundations of a society. But in themselves the myths are scientific. And, like religion, science is not an avenue for seeking power but a means of knowing.

Myth, I say, is the progenitor of science. Myth is alpha and omega, genealogy and teleology. Myths have always been scientific, and science as we know it derives from (or expresses) a Christian myth. (As I have indicated elsewhere, I mean by myth a creative response made by a community to what it considers supernatural truth. The term does not of course imply falsehood.) Within the Christian revelation, as it gradually entered into culture and was acted upon by multiple imaginations, certain elements provided "givens" necessary to the development of modern science. A respect for physical things and for the body as having significance, a conviction that the mind can know physical reality, and above all a belief that creation is good found their expression in scientific experimentation. Further, the methods of science grew up in close analogy to Christian philosophy and theology.

Science has its dogma, which came to be recognized in the same manner as dogma in theology. A belief becomes operative in the people who are concerned with the subject and in time becomes a ratified principle beyond the evidence of sensory data. Indeed, many times belief causes sensory data to be adjusted to conform to the principle. Conservation of energy is a prime example of this sort of dogma. At one stage in the history of science considerable debate centered on the validity of the conservation of energy. It was not at this time that the conservation principle became dogma, however, but later. Over a period of years the principle was seen to apply to a number of circumstances and became generally accepted. Then James Joule made an extensive survey of the relation of heat to energy, carrying around long, very sensitive thermometers to measure the temperature of water above and below waterfalls, constructing a water mill and other devices to measure the energy input and the heat output of the system. Subsequently the principle became well-fixed as a cornerstone of science. Einstein's theory of special relativity drew upon this concept and bolstered it. Now we simply do not allow the conservation principle to be violated. For example, some years ago it was discovered that energy and momentum were not conserved in beta decay—a form of radioactivity in which an atom changes by emitting an electron from the nucleus and, after shedding a gamma ray, becoming a stable

172 • UNBINDING PROMETHEUS

atom farther up the atomic scale. When this reaction turned out not to conserve energy and momentum, another particle was postulated, invisible, impossible to detect by any direct means, but nevertheless existing on the strength of belief. This particle, the neutrino, so small that it could possibly sail through the sun without touching an atom, was invented to account for the missing energy and momentum and at the same time balance out spin in a decay reaction. It would appear to be a questionable tactic thus to imagine an "ad hoc" entity, but the uses of the hypothesis are so great that it warrants the stratagem. And by this accommodation the foundations of science remain unshaken.

Admittedly, it would be possible to approach the structure of scientific knowledge as though it were only happily in coincidence with reality, in the manner of Leibnitz's monads. Or we could say that, since in mathematical manipulations we can always axiomatically conserve any desired property, we choose to make use of only those properties that correspond to physical observation. This kind of skeptical thinking is useful; but in actuality, both in classical and contemporary physics, we make use of principles as if they are expressing something real and consider axioms deduced from them to be expressing more or less accurately something about nature. I take this kind of thinking to be scholastic, perhaps even Thomistic, or perhaps more in the line of the subtle doctor, Duns Scotus. It seems no accident, at any rate, that scientific thinking assumed its characteristic forms under thirteenth-century Christian thinkers, whether Dominican or Franciscan is of no great moment. Science proved to be the most viable continuance of scholasticism, and even today the popular though now outmoded conception of science as a set of laws and provable facts is probably a somewhat diluted heritage of the schoolmen.

Essentially science is a contemplative operation. Scientific experimentation goes on in the mind. Laboratories are necessary before and after the true experiment, but they never provide a direct observation of the point in question. Only very rarely do the instruments rejoice, so to say, in announcing an immediate confirmation of a theory. Usually only long after readings are in and data reshaped and graphed does the form of an experiment take on a mental shape and give rise to the excitement of discovery. Experiment without imagination, without theory, tells us nothing. Nuclear fission, for example, was "observed" but not discovered by one of the great physicists, Enrico Fermi, some years before it was "discovered" by Lisa Meitner. Away from the laboratory, she fell to thinking about some strange results her colleague Otto Hahn had recorded, and within her imagination fission occurred, making what was strange into the familiar.

Science is always closely related to the current beliefs and desires of a society. Contemporary science began at the end of the Victorian Age when society was undergoing a marked change in all its modes of thought. The great so-called "classical" age in physics, which began with the early Renaissance, culminated about 1890 with the immense triumph of electromagnetic theory. But hardly had the theories of Maxwell and the seemingly accidental confirmation by Hertz come into being before Max Planck, in studying electromagnetic radiation from the sun, stumbled upon a new fundamental constant. As a result, the idea of the continuum, with its possibility for infinitely precise measurements, would give way to a basic uncertainty. The atom, which was then a chemical concept, would become physically definable, structured and discrete; and the new electromagnetism would take up its existence as photons. The discrete nature of experience which the Uncertainty Principle announced has characterized the age beginning at the turn of the century. It is this innovation in information, the idea of the quantum of energy, which led to the innovation in power

174 . UNBINDING PROMETHEUS

(atomic energy and fusion), to the polymerization of plastics and other new materials, and indirectly through automation to space travel. Each of the ways by which we characterize ages of civilization—materials, transportation, power, and information—received a new symbolic dimension, presented to it by a breakthrough in information. Information dominates our age and provides the scientific aspect of the myth.

The present age is one of structuralizing, but it produces a quite different set of structures from the mechanistic, continuous constructions of the past. An awareness of finiteness permeates all our thinking today. The very fact of existence indicates the bound condition of matter. Objects exist as entities because they lack the energy to come apart. Since chaos is above us in the energy scale, every entity falls into a particular existence state through a sacrifice of energy. Because existence is bound, it occurs only at discrete levels, as a violin string vibrates only in sub-multiples of its length. The states are distinct and frequently well-separated. An entity can make a transition from one state to another, but no progression takes place through the interval. Frequently we must suppose, as a matter of fact, that it does not exist between these states. There is simply existence in one state and then existence in another. This strange model is most apparent in any exploration of light emitted from atoms.

Such cellularized sensibility is an important element of the scientific myth of our day. Although we continue to ascribe to fact the central role in meaning which has been characteristic of the past few centuries, in the sub-microscopic world fact is no longer the history of individual events and therefore not the causal consequence of a willed act. Fact is rather the distribution of cell occupancy according to the principles of probability. In probability theory, if many identical events are observed, the outcomes will range over a set of possibilities. The percentage that will result in any one possibility can be fairly well predicted, but the outcome of any single event can-not be foretold. The distribution of probabilities, not the description of an event, constitutes information.

I am, of course, greatly exaggerating the implications of uncertainty. There are acts of choice, of arbitrary interven-tion, of designed purpose, which set up the probability distribution. But human will is seemingly not an agent con-trolling an exact causal mechanism. Certainly the will is as operative and as free as ever, but the mechanism itself has been discovered to have some inbuilt waywardness.

The idea of meaning undergoes a change in such a situa-tion. In effect, meaning is put aside as much as possible, and information becomes the central concern. In the last several decades an interesting and fruitful field called information science has arisen which treats information in the manner of thermodynamics. The modern computer is the instrument—the laboratory—of this science, and communications is its subject. This process is ostensibly value-free; it does not evaluate the messages it communicates. Inevitably it becomes part of the myth, however, and is subject to the overall pur-poses of a society. Modern philosophers might do well to tangle with the work of information scientists, perhaps not so much because of the direct epistemology involved as because of the metaphysics it represents.

Let me turn to our categories of technology. The distribu-tion of energy has always had enormous effects on history. There are "have and have-not" nations in terms of coal and oil, with the have-nots being at considerable disadvantage. Although new reservoirs of oil continue to be found, it is ob-vious that the supply of fossil fuels is finite. And since the consumption of energy has been rising exponentially to the effect that we consume in a few years more than in all past history, then the possible reserves can last only a matter of years—perhaps as much as a hundred. This situation will result in a rapid and violent reshuffling of political alignments if no new sources of power become available. But of course we now have atomic energy.

The story of atomic energy is one of accelerated scientific development into technology, running from Planck's quantum in 1900 to Einstein's special relativity in 1905 and the splitting of the atom in 1932 to the discovery of fission in 1939. At this point technology set out on what was surely the most massive development ever undertaken, the making of the atomic bomb. The development of power reactors began a decade later, and now almost fifty years after the discovery of fission a number of good-sized atomic reactor generating plants are in place. There are not enough of them, to be sure, and their operation is expensive and under considerable criticism from the public. But they are sufficient to indicate that we can extend the world's energy supply by another hundred years or so. A good share of France's energy is now generated by atomic reactors. However, the supply of uranium, like coal and oil, is limited and unequally distributed; even the possibilities of breeding additional fuel by neutron activation has finite extensions. The political predicament created by the necessities of power consumption, then, is not solved by atomic energy.

One supply of energy not limited to any great degree in its geographic distribution is water. The possibility of gaining tremendous power from hydrogen is evident in the hydrogen bomb. Fusion is the most natural source of power in the universe—the energy, as a matter of fact, of stars. Unfortunately, however, the minimum size for a good fusion generator seems to be about that of the moon. Attempts to confine in a small volume the necessary energy for controlled fusion have not been successful thus far, although we always seem to be on the verge of a radically new development in this containment. The problem is difficult: whereas fission started with a controlled reaction and *advanced* to an explosion, the first induced fusion reaction *was* an explosion, the H-bomb with an atomic bomb at its core. We shall no doubt solve the fusion problem, and sources of power can then be distributed all over the world. If so, the necessity for aggressive actions to obtain new sources of power will be alleviated. Unfortunately, however, the discrepancy between have and have-not countries may only be emphasized by this new energy source, since fusion power centers are likely to be enormous, requiring tremendous financial investments in plants and distribution systems. The maldistribution of excess wealth and of brain power will be emphasized by the new dimensions of nuclear energy.

The magnitude of facilities for atomic energy, fission or fusion, obviously leads toward centralization and federalization, toward states rather than cities. Another direction of development in power may tend, however, towards individualization and small units of social structure. The necessity for portability, emphasized by space travel (and illustrated by the teenager's ever-present solid state radio), has induced the development of miniaturization; we are exploiting the possibility of using for useful purposes very little power, supplied by small rechargeable units or improved dry cells. The advances have been largely chemical applications rather than physical ones; when we learn to exploit the energy by which atoms are bound to surfaces, we may be able to reduce the weight of batteries by as much as thirty times—enough to allow the continuance of a highly mobile society with individual automobiles even after the supply of petroleum is exhausted.

Solar power can play a significant role in small portable devices, as it does for the hand-held calculator, but no apparent way has been discerned for the sun to supply the large-scale high-density power volumes demanded by an affluent society. Solar energy seems likely to continue playing a minor role in the energy situation.

The state of affairs for materials is much like that for energy: rich natural deposits will be exhausted. Plastics derived from petroleum will be rare. Yet we are not likely to be living in an economy of scarcity. If society demands affluence, which means at its root abundant energy, then materials will not be a barrier. Miniaturization, which comes in the guise of improvement, will diminish the quantity demanded; ceramics and bio-mass will supplement supply. Style will adjust itself to availability.

What is evident in all these adjustments is the central role of technology. Mere skills are of no great consequence. The lore that has been passed down from parent to child will serve purposes of pleasure, not survival. The hard core of existence, that which produces food, clothing, and shelter, will be handled by technology, with relatively few people involved. So, too, for the next few layers of the social structure that provide conveniences, comforts, and luxuries. The great industrial system, the triumphant accomplishment of the past two centuries, will still turn out its products but will make use of few people, as agriculture already does, having made the transition almost a century before. The so-called service sector can take up little of the slack; it is itself subject to automation, as the automobile service stations demonstrate. Massive unemployment will result unless society can conceive imaginative solutions to the economic problems. If the proper adjustments can be made, the bulk of the "labor" force will be employed in what we regard as "quality of life." People will work with the system, not for it. They will develop their own innovations, fitting them into the general structure. Present ideas of productivity and wealth will need to undergo radical change, but the flexibility of a free society should allow the new conditions to be worked out. Transition to a new epoch will be difficult and exceedingly dangerous, but beyond the risky passage should lie smooth seas and auspicious gales.

My attempt here has been to lay out a measure of how technology will affect the polis of the future. At the base of my analysis is an assumption of ample energy. Two other scenarios are possible. One is to set aside the desire for affluence and live at the level consistent with the energy that can be garnered from the sun; and, though the simplicity implied has much appeal, such a life would not be comfortable or secure. The other plan is not a plan at all: to go ahead with as much determination as we can muster, just as we have been doing, letting the instabilities mount until the whole system topples. The crash, however, is likely to be disastrous. What has been forced upon us at the end of the twentieth century is the awareness that civilization is inevitably dependent upon technology. Some acknowledgement of the bastard child seems called for if the family line is to endure. For the ineluctable truth is that, recognized for what it is and given its proper due, in technology lies the hope for a free and prosperous society.

13

The Rise of the
Quantitative World View

For the past sixty or seventy years historians of science have attempted without complete success to destroy the myth that modern science rose quite suddenly with Galileo and came to full flower within a century in the work of Newton. The uses of that myth have been cultural and perhaps psychological in an age exalting physics over metaphysics. It is quite likely a human tendency to attribute to great men those changes which in reality arise disparately and unobtrusively throughout an age of transition. It has been peculiarly a modern tendency, however, to see those men as martyrs who stand *against* their age, enemies of bigotry and ignorance. This kind of interpretation of Galileo, Bruno, and others has accorded them credit not wholly justified and in the process rather seriously distorted the history of science. In our century, however, Lynn Thorndike, George Sarton, A. C. Crombie, and others have shown that the rise of science in the seventeenth century was not simply the work of a few heroes, but was well prepared for.

Despite the fabled account, experiment did not begin with Galileo's dropping balls from the Leaning Tower of Pisa. Even if that story is not apocryphal, the fact is that the same experiment was performed some years before—about 1570—when Simon Steven of Flanders dropped weights from a window down to a sounding board. Such experiments—dependent upon the recognition of qualities, rather than the measurement of quantities—may have been more common in the sixteenth century than our extant documents indicate. Indeed, the many speculations on motion which have been preserved from that period do not seem wholly divorced from observation. But even quantitative experiments were underway. Scientific investigations of the declination of the compass had begun by 1525 with the work of Felipe Gullen and was carried on by Pedro Nunez, Joao de Castro, and others. A century earlier, about 1450, Giovanni da Fontana performed careful experiments with rockets. Professor Crombie makes a good case for the origin of experimental science as early as 1250, with Robert Grosseteste, at Oxford. One suspects that the rise of experimental science may have been engendered by an evolving technology which required deliberate experimentation for practical purposes and that in the process excesses of skill allowed leeway for curiosity. When an adequate account of technology is available, we are likely to find a continuous history of experiment with many instances of independent investigation.

If experiment did not begin with Galileo, neither did physical theory begin with him, even though a modern physicist, Robert Lindsay, in admitting that Galileo was not a notable experimentalist, writes "but he is the founder of Theoretical Physics, and that is fame enough for any man." It is true that from Galileo on there has been continuous sequential development of theoretical physics, thanks in part to his witty pen, to the printing press, and to his two brilliant disciples. But to give him credit as the founder of theoretical physics is to overlook not only the contemporaneous claim of Kepler but the whole series of thinkers during the Renaissance who developed the idea of impetus, extending back at least to Olbert of Saxony in the fourteenth century. The Mertonian Rule, which states that bodies with uniform acceleration increase their velocities by equal amounts in equal intervals of time, was used by William of Heytesbury and others at Oxford late in the fourteenth century; and the relation of acceleration to distance was worked out in detail by the Spanish Scholastic Dominico Soto about 1570. It would be surprising if these are the studies Galileo dismisses as "superficial observations" in his introduction to the "Third Day" of his *Two New Sciences*; but it would be even more surprising if a man of his learning and position were ignorant of these studies which concern the very key to the Galilean ideas of motion. The construct of motion as the interconnection of time with space was a recurring tool for physical thought as is evidenced by frequent references to the earth's motion and rotation before Copernicus—for example, the theories of Buridan and Nicolás Oresme. And when one looks back through Simplicius, Hipparchus, and Aristarchus to Aristotle, it would seem that whatever the case we might make for the fairly modern onset of experimentation, we should have to admit a very ancient beginning for theoretical physics.

What did arise in the late Middle Ages and throughout the Renaissance was a concern for precision of measurement beyond the demands of practicality or profit. The thesis I wish to explore is that it was the development of the metrological process—the concept of measure for its own sake—arising during the Renaissance, that engendered the cultural shift from a qualitative to a quantitative world view—to what Alfred North Whitehead has called "the characteristic scientific philosophy which closed the 17th century."

Measure concerns primarily time, mass, and length. The instrument of measuring time was the clock, invented late in the thirteenth century. This device was to give rise to a school of fine craftsmen which, to this day, provides artisans to build instruments of precision. It induced the full development of gears and the perfection of the screw. On quite another level, it provided a satisfactory analogue for a deistic conception of the universe which was to lend itself handily to the new astronomy, even Kepler making use of the comparison. But it was in making time an independent entity, no longer the private tool of astronomers, that the clock was to have its most important historical effect. The old variable hours, organic, related to human needs and marked by the offices of worship, were now replaced by precise fractions of an inexorable cycle, portioned out by a mechanism not made in the image of man. The infinite divisibility of such a uniform continuum became easily imaginable. The idea of precision seized the popular imagination sufficiently enough that the terminology of minute and second became common in the fourteenth century. Thus, Geoffrey of Beaux reported the lunar eclipse of March 18, 1345, as 3h29m54s—a calculated result, of course, but one showing how precision had affected thought. In the next century Fontana postulated for the purpose of scientific experiment a clock with a dial rotating in a minute and another dial rotating once a second. The idea of a countably infinite divisibility was obviously present. Early clocks generally had a frenum which controlled the time of the escape mechanism, and this frenum determined a beat of once every two seconds, its pace fixing the least-count of the instrument. These clocks were large weight-driven devices, but in the latter part of the fifteenth century spring-wound clocks made available a portable timepiece. Although the clepsydra, a device for measuring the flow of water, remained the chief instrument for measuring short intervals of time, the perfection of the watch during the sixteenth century was bringing a better device to hand.

The idea of precision in the determination of mass has a very practical aspect; in fact, there are early records of city ordinances legislating honest weights. Alchemy, too, encouraged precise measurement of mass, but records show that in the sixteenth century the idea of precision in weighing had become independent of its utilitarian value. Simon Steven proposed a decimal system for weights in his *De Thienda* of 1585, but before this time, about 1557, as Cyril Smith has pointed out an assayer in Wittenberg named Schreitmann described and apparently made a decimal set of weights. They were little helical wire bits, the smallest of which he called atoms. "These must be so small," said Schreitmann, "that no balance, however quick and true it may be, will detect one, two, three, or four of them but needs ten to produce a moderate deflection." Schreitmann's atoms turn out to be a little less than a milligram; apparently the best balance he was aware of had a sensitivity of a few milligrams, and recent experiments of balances of that time confirm this sensitivity. But by 1579 Ercher suggests that a good balance should respond to a "quintlein"—about a quarter of a milligram. This discrepancy by a factor of twenty does not seem to be an accidental variation but, rather, evidence of a rapid increase in sensitivity of instruments during the intervening score of years. The imaginative use of precise weighing in the curious scientific investigation of matter became possible with the increase in practical measure of mass and the organization of these measurements in a decimal system—a development of the sixteenth century.

The increase in precision of measuring short lengths is less easy to document to a time prior to the seventeenth century. The need for high precision generally would await the advent of interchangeable parts, but there was one endeavor which quite early demanded replaceable parts: armaments. It was necessary to have moderately uniform bores to guns and a consistent diameter to shot if armies were to operate efficiently. The *calibre* of shot became the *caliper* of measure. Apparently the first mention in English of the word *caliper* is a treatise of 1588 on the *Art of Shooting*, in which we are told to "measure first with a pair of caliper compasses the whole thickness of the piece." A fine pair of compasses is included in Holbein's painting, "The Ambassadors," in 1533, but since the points are not turned inward or outward as they would be for calipers, this instrument is apparently intended for the drawing board. The compass is an old instrument of practical use in masonry and a precision instrument in geometry; it was adapted to the precise measurements of physical objects in the fifteenth or sixteenth century.

The ability to read a measurement with high precision depends on the turning of a screw or the aligning of a vernier. The screw itself dates from about 400 B. C. But the invention of the lathe for making screws belongs to the early sixteenth century; there is a careful drawing by Leonardo da Vinci of a screw-cutting lathe. The screws cut on such a lathe could be more finely threaded and more uniform than the hand-manufactured screws preceding them so that their use as measuring devices would be possible—even probable. Gascoigne's Micrometer of 1637 which employed the screw to move a wire at the focal point of a telescope appears a rather complex device to have come into existence full blown. It seems likely that it was preceded by a more straightforward use of the screw as a measuring device. In any case, the precision screws which made the device possible began to be made by Leonardo's contemporaries.

As for the vernier, the astrolabe or the quadrant would seem to be a fitting instrument for its introduction. In the Holbein painting showing the compass is also a table version of a double-quadrant, which one is tempted to interpret as having a vernier, for it evidences a 40-degree span coinciding with 45-degree markings. The ring does not appear to move, however; consequently the markings must be interpreted as a version of the shadow-square which had its trigonometric uses on the astrolabe. Nonetheless, we need not leave Pierre Vernier's invention of 1631 without antecedents. In 1542 Pedro Nunez described his attempt to divide degrees into 90 parts by scribing successive quarter circles and marking them so that 90 divisions of the first circle correspond to 89 divisions of the second, 88 divisions of the third, etc. After attempting to make use of this scheme in 1587, Tycho Brahe discarded it as not worth the trouble. But it continued to be used experimentally, and in the hands of Clavius and Curtius about the end of the sixteenth century, it reached a perfection which led naturally to the movable device of Vernier.

The measurement of length on any large scale becomes the measurement of angle. The sixteenth century was the great age of surveying and of cartography. An illustration of a surveying instrument known as the polymetrium apparently by Waldseemuller, the cartographer who named America, appeared in a 1512 edition of the *Margarita Philosophica*. Many more surveying instruments came into use in the same century, including the theodolite of Leonard Digges in England in 1571. Since the precise location of various landmarks became a matter of great interest during the period, the enthusiasm for cartography spread from Saint Die, where Waldseemuller was located, over the Continent rather generally, to find a great center in the Netherlands. If I may return for a moment to the Holbein picture, there is here a very excellent example of the torquetum, which appears to be adapted for surveying. In fact, I should hazard a guess that the two ambassadors of the picture, the bishop and the nobleman, were cartographers—the drawing compass, the square, the globe, the charts, the multi-facet sundial, as well as the torquetum and quadrant, indicating such a connection. But my concern at the moment is one of measurement, and I should say that the interest in precise cartography during the sixteenth century exceeded the requirements of immediate use.

One final point should be made about precision. That is that precision in the making of measurement and precision in the recognition of qualities have quite different effects on the human sensibility. A concern for appearance remains, in essence, a concern with qualities, so that the precision of a Holbein, a Michelangelo, a Galileo, is a natural outgrowth of

Scholastic and nominalist philosophy—a flowering of the Middle Ages in the Renaissance. Galileo's concern was unmistakably with the quality of things; he reported to us not the data of his experiments, but his conclusions; he designed a telescope which would see the features of the moon right side up but could not be used for measuring as could, for example, the telescope with the inverted image built according to Kepler's design. To Galileo, the perfection of the circle outweighed Kepler's measurement of elliptic orbits. Despite all his talk of measure and all his urging of new inventions, Galileo was a scholastic philosopher standing in the Age of Science. For the scientific age had already begun—and if we must find a representative figure for it, that figure is Tycho Brahe. With him metrological precision did not stem from new inventions but from a desire for precision itself. He had large instruments made—six feet in radius, fifteen feet in radius—however large he needed to gain the precision he desired. He accomplished a hundred-fold gain in precision. It was not his theories which were important—not his speculation, but his practice—the numbers he took down. Tycho Brahe, stubborn, egotistical, wrongheaded, perhaps not very bright, and not at all a hero, carefully measured and carefully reported his measurements. And here was the new precision —the factual, non-sensible abstraction of measure. The idea of gaining facts by measurement had taken form; for better or worse, it was the paradoxical gift of the great humanistic epoch—the Renaissance.

14

Science, History, and the Evidence of Things Not Seen

A FEW YEARS BACK, a physicist in Rumania began an article with a statement which illuminated, quite unintentionally, the entire discipline of physics. "One of the most remarkable facts in the field of weak interaction physics," he wrote, "is the non-observation of bosonic leptons." The note was in *Physical Review Letters*, a little journal that reports the latest scientific discoveries to an expectant, highly specialized audience almost on an emergency basis. To most people, no doubt, a fact of non-observation would seem to be the stuff of which satire, not science, is made. And, as it happened, the note appeared at the same time that one of our most prominent cartoonists was depicting a somewhat Aristophanic sequence: the people of his mythical kingdom were lining up for days to not-see the country's greatest treasure, the "bashful blobolink," whose appearances were so brief as to be invisible, though no one doubted his existence. Satire, of course, has many edges, and may at any moment slice through inadvertently to a basic truth. It could indeed be true, as the cartoonist may or may not have intended to imply, that a country's greatest treasure is something that its people can not-see. It is, after all, the grace of office, not a naked man, that resides inside the Emperor's clothes. And though the modern physicist is frequently reproached for admitting to his ken only entities whose existence can be demonstrated, he is insensitive to the importance of the non-observation of the bosonic lepton.

A lepton is a light elementary particle which responds to the "weak force" (one of the four fundamental forces—the others being the gravitational, the electromagnetic, and the "strong"). Muons, electrons, and neutrinos are leptons which have been "observed"; but they are not bosons—they are fermions, that is, they obey the Fermi-Dirac statistics of the exclusion principle, according to which no more than one can occupy any given set of quantum numbers. Bosons obey Bose-Einstein statistics not limited by the exclusion principle. A photon is bosonic, but is not a lepton. The Rumanian physicist quoted earlier was saying that theory allows for the existence of a particle responding to the weak force which does not obey the exclusion principle, but that so far it has not been observed.

The explanation does not greatly diminish the urge to satire. Before indulging it, however, we should remind ourselves that non-observation has a long and honored career among scientists. The most memorable of the events of non-observation was the "failure" of the Michelson-Morley experiment in 1887 to measure the drift of the earth through ether. Actually, what was not observed was any change in the apparent velocity of light caused by the addition of the earth's motion to that of light in the ether. H. A. Lorentz suggested (1892) that the velocity actually did change but that the length of all measuring devices contracted in the direction of motion just sufficiently to obscure the change. Einstein took a simpler but more daring approach (1905) by *postulating* a uniform velocity of light for all observers, regardless of their states of motion. The consequence of this egalitarian postulate was the special theory of relativity, according to which the length of a moving body does, indeed, contract in the direction of motion, and time dilates as well; but the velocity of light stays the same. The fact that change was not observed was, to Einstein, evidence that change did not occur.

The null result of a crucial experiment is, of course, an important event, although its importance, indeed its cruciality, does not become fixed until some simplifying postulate changes the world view. History, in a sense, ordains the experiment—in truth, captures it as material for its own discipline. For a time the experiment exists in science as part of the logical structure leading to the postulate; but soon the positive results of the new manner of thought take over the task of authenticating its reality, and the experiment itself, no longer needed, falls away from the coherent and active body of knowledge that is science. The "special history" of science preserves the story of the experiment as a memorable anecdote for use in the psychology of innovation, or for whatever other purpose it might serve in the pursuit of other disciplines in the *speculum mentis*. But its original utility in the science is gone. For unlike most other disciplines, science is residual, not accretional, and this characteristic gives it a kind of primitive innocence.

The nomenclature of physics commemorates its saints—an Ampere of current, a Volt of potential difference, a Faraday of capacitance, a Coulomb of charge, Newton's laws, Maxwell's equations, Planck's constant—the litany is extensive. Such piety bespeaks a concern for the past and a desire for its conservation. But these marks of deference are more memorials than *memoria*, monuments to the past rather than its preservation. The reason for this anti-historical bent lies in the nature of scientific discovery: discoveries of science are generally not contained in an artifact. No critical return to an original text is likely to reveal a further truth, nor will it deepen the understanding of a principle, as it does, say, for a poem or a painting. Certainly a scientific model exists once the discovery is made; but it exists in a communal imagination, not in a single work of art. It is discovered, not revealed

—even in ambiguity. The model, not the incident of its discovery, is open to exploration. Only the residue of discovery remains.

Fame of neither sort awaits the leptonic writing cited at the beginning of this paper. The non-observation of the bosonic lepton as reported in the scientific journal is not the outcome of a crucial experiment; it is, rather, an observation on the part of a theorist of a lack of expected findings in experimental data. The theorist goes on to comment that evidence such as he seeks may actually be present in experiments already performed, unnoticed by investigators. Such an oversight would not be unique in the annals of physics; the great physicist Enrico Fermi did not discover fission because he did not imagine it, though the evidence was before him. Awareness of the facts alone did not constitute "observation" of the phenomenon. What it is that sets the imagination going in a certain direction is not easily ascertained, but one of its progenitors is surely a *theme*—an activated postulate, a possible idea—in its local culture, local in the sense of a current community of like-minded scholars.

Gerald Holton speaks of the effect of thematic commitment on explanation, noting the way in which pertinent themes are subject to a prevailing style. As an example, he points to the recurring reversals in the causal relation of chaos and order. Kinetic theory (1860) explains pressure as the elastic bumping of molecules moving in random fashion against a surface—order out of chaos; but Einstein's account (1905) of the Brownian movement explains the seeming randomness of molecular motion as the result of a great number of quite predictable collisions—chaos out of order. The uncertainty principle (1927) again reverses the roles. Similarly, Holton points to the frequent reversals of commitment to a view of reality as either continuous or discrete, particles or waves being alternately in style. He has identified fifty such themes in the physical sciences and supposes that the total number is

not much greater. In thus mapping out his field of explanation, Holton illustrates a physicist's preference in style for a
theme of normal coordinates—if he is in the continuous mode
—or a set of quantum numbers—if he is in the discrete. Even
with so modest a set as fifty binary choices, Holton would
have available some million billion variations, which one
would suppose to be adequate.

Whether the style at any one time limits or frees the imagination is a matter of speculation. No age can anticipate a
future epoch except the one it is busy preparing. Such ideas as
atomicity and continuity may alternate in style from age to
age, but even so, Democritus' atom, despite the verbal similarity, was not the progenitor of the current model. The concept had to arise out of contemporaneous material. The atom
worked its way up from Dalton through chemistry, found a
sort of confirmation in Maxwell's kinetic theory of gases,
gained components through Thompson's electron and
Rutherford's nucleus, was structuralized by Bohr's model,
became sophisticated with wave mechanics, then spallated
into elementary particles—all in about a century and a half.
An earlier age, one can speculate, could not have conceived
of such a development, would not have accepted what we
now take for experimental evidence as actual observation.
The chain of evidence has indeed been indirect, sometimes
remote. Even the most direct and irrefutable evidence seems
somewhat nebulous: the track in a cloud chamber, for instance, which an observer or a camera sees as the reflection of
light from droplets of moisture formed on ions remaining
along a path supposedly followed by the electron or other
charged particles. That evidence is fairly "hard," as data go.
Uncharged particles leave no such track. The observation of
uncharged particles, therefore, is of a more removed order: it
is obtained by filling in unseen bits of data in agreement with
conservation principles—the substance of things hoped for,
the evidence of things not seen. The faith of a medieval

scientist would not likely have been up to an act such as not-seeing elementary particles, any more than a modern investigator can not-see angels. The themes are different.

Angels have fled the imagination of men who find no utility in their presences. We can no longer turn a stone "and start a wing." There was a time, however, when an elaborate angelology gave rise to heated debate of theoretical questions.

The well-established nine choirs with their three hierarchies are in fact the product of angelologists, though the names of the choirs occur in Scripture and the arrangement is partly exegetical. Both Dante and Thomas Aquinas follow Dionysius, the Pseudo-Areopagite, in placing in the highest category the Seraphim, the Cherubim, and the Thrones; in the second the Dominations, the Virtues, and the Powers; and in the third the Principalities, the Archangels, and the Angels—with man a little lower. Angelologists did not seem to carry out serious investigations of distinguishing characteristics of the various choirs; for example, the debate continues even now whether St. Michael the Archangel was not, in fact, a Seraph.

Do angels observe an exclusion principle? The number that can occupy the head of a pin might lead one to think that angels, like photons, are bosons, observing no exclusion principle —as one might suspect from their identification with light. Of course, these particular angels might be only one class of angels—those of the host of angels which are indistinguishable from one another.

The tenet of angelic indistinguishability is not supported by authority: in the 1950 Encyclical *Humani Generis*, Pius XII chides theologians who cast doubt on the personhood of angels. Only three angels, however, are officially allowed names: Michael, Gabriel, and Raphael. Other names which occur in apocryphal works and rabbinical literature—and were used by Milton—were rejected by Pope Zachary in 745 and again by a synod at Aix-la-Chapelle in 789. Lacking names, the angels also lack individual characteristics that would cause an exchange of assignments among them to be noticed. It is in this sense that they are taken here to be indistinguishable.

Thomas reasoned that each angel was of a different species —that angels are as different from one another as cats are from dogs. The Schoolmen accepted Thomas's authority on this matter. The argument was not persuasive to the Scotists, however, who continued to believe that all angels are of one species, nor to the followers of Suarez, who held several species to exist. Judging from the depiction of angels in works of art, one would suppose the popular belief favored the Scotist position.

Guardian angels are, likely enough, indistinguishable in a technical sense, but since they do have exclusive assignments in our parallel system they would have to be fermions. The special assignment of these angels, with a Scriptural basis in Daniel and a usefulness in lullabies, was generally accepted up to the Renaissance but came under question by some of the later angelologists, depending, as Holton might put it, on what theme each was following—the Protestant camp rather disliking the possibility of intervention between man and maker. Milton's angels, one might recall, stayed in Heaven except for the two messengers to the Garden, Raphael and Michael.

The corporeality of angels, like that of neutrinos, was another matter not easily settled. The probability that they had mass seemed to overlap zero. In the end, the weight of the evidence, as for neutrinos, favored no mass. In such a circumstance arose the question of how angels could be seen, as they were from time to time; it was suggested by Aquinas that the angels themselves could not be seen, but that they caused a condensation of clouds which reflected light in a shape that would have meaning for the observer. Usually angels were not seen but were known by their effect on observable things.

Angels had their anti-particles in the fallen angels. A good conservation principle operating at the time of the separation of the good and the bad would have set up as many minuses as pluses, which would have made for sounder drama—the outcome of the battle in Heaven would have seemed to be in more doubt—but the opportunity was, apparently, overlooked; prevailing opinion held for about a third as many bad angels as good ones. Neither does there seem to be any record of the two coming together to annihilate each other in a burst of glory as anti-particles should, although, with some shifting of suppositions, the concept might have had appeal.

It is difficult to be objective about the myth in which one lives. B. M. G. Reardon has commented:

> Myth appears as an organic function of the culture within which it occurs. . . . In the beginning myth is a mode of existence, an integration of thought, feeling, and action. It may acquire expression in words, but only as these are pointers to a concrete reality. For a myth is lived—and projected ritually—before ever it begins to be clearly thought about . . . [being] in its primary state . . . not so much the object of thought as its condition.

The myth of fact so engulfs the present that reality itself often becomes obscured. Extensive and fanciful constructions are frequently put forth in speculative disciplines under the guise of fact and in the trappings of science. Jacques Barzun has warned the historian against this danger, particularly in the use of pseudo-facts imported from other disciplines. Jose Ortega y Gasset, writing forty years before, says quite flatly, "By themselves, facts do not give us reality."

These two sages have both concerned themselves with the relation of history to science and seemingly have reached quite opposite evaluations. Barzun concludes that science and history are totally other; "the substance of history, we know, is not amenable to measurement in the scientific sense. . . ." He identifies science with method: "in science the elements are clear, abstract, and unchangeable. . . . Because of this clarity and fixity, it is easy to use these concepts correctly once their strange artificiality has been firmly grasped; it is then but the application of a method." The elements of history, on the other hand, he indicates, elude definition and consequently no historical method can exist. "Obviously, the two modes of thought do not mix well; there are no natural transitions from the one to the other, the movement of the mind in each goes counter to the other."

Ortega, on the contrary, views physics as the norm of modern knowledge for all disciplines—history in particular. This opinion, diametrically opposed to Barzun's, arises from a difference of understanding about science and about history. Ortega sees science as sister to poetry because of its imaginative character:

> In order to discover reality we must for a moment lay aside the facts that surge about us, and remain alone with our minds. Then we construct an imaginary reality, a pure invention of our own; then, following in solitude the guidance of our imagining, we find what aspect, what visible shapes, in short, what facts will produce that imaginary reality.

It is then, Ortega says, that we compare the observed facts with our imagined ones, and if they "mate happily," we have discovered reality.

This process of discovery, as described by Ortega, has been recounted frequently by scientists. Often, when the imagination has given the correct shape of the concept, a snap of recognition occurs so that the scientist is quite certain what the data will tell him long before he sees them. There is a rightness about the concept, just as there is about a true line of poetry, which gives to its discoverer a certainty and a deep satisfaction. The role of facts prior to this act of the imagination is ambiguous; the facts indicate the problem, as Ortega noted, and set the imagination in motion, but the facts then retire from the scene; discovery is by no means a process of induction by method from facts.

Now this kind of science, which Ortega is describing, is the science of discovery and, as Thomas Kuhn points out, is quite different from normal science. In his consideration of ordinary and extraordinary science, Kuhn first establishes a modern schoolman's outlook: "If science is the constellation of facts, theories, and methods collected in current texts, then scientists are the men who, successfully or not, have striven to contribute one or another element of that particular constellation." This picture of science supposes an "ever-growing stockpile" of technique and knowledge which results from scientific development. What Kuhn calls normal science is somewhat more imaginative than this textbook science, but it partakes of the same methodical character. Discovery, on the other hand, violates the methods of its time; it is deeply intuitive, highly non-systematic. Because of the residual nature of science, the results of discovery—the revolutions in science, Kuhn calls them—sink finally into ordinary science and become part of method. It is this afterview of discovery sunk into normal science that Barzun is describing when he states, " . . . genius in science consists in adding to the stock of . . . defined entities and showing their place and meaning within the whole system of science and number." At any one time, this ordinary science appears to the outside observer complete and efficient. These characteristics tempt other disciplines to model themselves upon ordinary science, mistaking efficiency for genius. Barzun rejects the method of this science for his model of the discipline of history. It is, of course, a different science from the one Ortega accepts as his model.

Ortega sees in physics a habit of the intuitive mind grasping phenomena and building an imaginary construction, then checking for conformity with reality at every observable point. It is this model of physics as a paradigm for other disciplines which he urges on historians. Other than in its identification with physics, Barzun has much the same model; associating history with intuitive thought, he declares that "genius in the realm of intuition consists in discovering pattern and significance in the uncontrollable confusion of life and embodying the discovery in intelligible form." The two views differ, certainly. Barzun does not suggest for the historian the *play* of the imagination which Ortega recognizes in the physicist. Indeed, this play might lead to the very danger of unwarranted assumptions and preposterous conclusions in the works of history against which Barzun inveighs. But the views are similar enough to be within the range of reconciliation.

Ortega is careful to point out that it is only in the habit of construction that he urges physics upon history: "The other characteristics of physics are not such as to be desirable for history." He views history as mission-oriented. "The primary and most elemental task of history is hermeneutic, which is to say interpretive," Ortega remarks, going on to point out that interpretation occurs in the very selection of facts to be arranged. Barzun maintains that interpretation is optional, and some histories can do without it. His criteria for history—narrative, chronology, concreteness, memorability—would not seem to be in conflict with Ortega's views except on the third point, for here the hermeneutical mission and his theory of generations bring Ortega close to abstractions. "The investigation of human lives is not possible," he claims, "if the wide variety in these animals does not hide an identical basic structure." To put it in other terms, for Ortega persons in the same generation evince a common aspect which allows them to be viewed as indistinguishable particles. Barzun is not so much on the side of the angels as of the Greek gods; for him, every event, every person must maintain his individual character. It is up to other disciplines to abstract what they will from the careful delineation of history.

Barzun and Ortega agree that history must be grasped intuitively, that patterns must be perceived if one is to make sense of history. For Ortega, the pattern is imagined, put together theoretically, then checked against observation. Barzun seeks in the midst of events a pattern that meets his criteria for genuine history. The two methods may result in equivalent patterns—indeed, are likely to do so, since history accounts for events which have actually happened rather than predicts events which may or may not happen. But only if the patterns are *inevitably* equivalent, as are those of Schrödinger's equations and Heisenberg's matrices for quantum mechanics, can one say that the choice of approaches is at the disposal of the historian—a matter of style. The possibilities for variance, however, are manifestly evident. Therefore a decision of legitimacy regarding the two approaches is, in a sense, crucial.

The utility of unseen presences is one of the points on which the two approaches are likely to differ. All ages have invisible agencies which they accept on non-empirical evidence. Angels are as much historical entities as are elementary particles, and the historian has the duty to treat both in a manner free of cynical enlightenment. But the employment of non-observable elements by the historian himself is suspect in the discipline of history. Admittedly, Ortega is as quick as Barzun to reject psychological interpretations of history, yet his hermeneutical method calls for the completion of imagined patterns by some means—invention if necessary, in the manner of physics.

Perhaps there are instances when the historian may legitimately use the second level of observation—the completion of a pattern by a process of imagined data. But to use physics as a paradigm for history would require further abstraction: the observation of unseen presences not only at the second level but at a third as well. The familiarly observable leptons seem to be truly elementary, but the far more numerous hadrons—the generally heavier particles, including protons and neutrons, which obey the strong nuclear force and many of which are observable only on the second level—exhibit structure and therefore are themselves apparently made up of components. These components have been christened "quarks," three of which seem to be necessary, each with a set of quantum numbers which, when assigned, account for the composition of all hadrons. However, in late 1974, two unexpected unseen hadrons were "observed," their existence requiring a fourth quark with a different set of quantum numbers, which, in the self-mocking patois of physicists at play, is said to have the property of *Charm*. As investigations proceed, it is not impossible that the levels could multiply and the quantum numbers increase until the possible variations outnumber the varieties on Holton's themes—indeed, justify the hypothesis of St. Thomas that each angel is a separate species.

Such constructions, in all their elaborateness, represent the appropriate operation of physics, whereas they do not seem to be legitimate for history. As intuitive and poetic as physics may be, it is not the right model for the discipline of history. The constructions of science are those which build a residual discipline. And history is, *par excellence*, accretional.

15

Scientific Discovery and Gratitude

MY TOPIC for this essay, Scientific Discovery and Gratitude, might best be addressed by a good phenomenological psychologist, someone more accustomed than a physicist to seeing into the psyche. But I undertake it because of a certainty that there is a basic truth in the connection of gratitude to science—something very fundamental to the act of discovery and always present but rarely observed. The early Greek physicist Archimedes may have said it all when he hopped out of the tub and ran down the street shouting "Eureka!" "I have found it" is, I believe, the translation usually carried in children's books on science.

Archimedes, as we remember, was commissioned to determine whether a king's crown was solid gold or merely plated. According to this undoubtedly apocryphal tale, he was quite stumped for a way of doing so without injuring the precious artifact—until he noticed that his own loss of weight in water was equal to the weight of the water displaced. Accordingly he could determine the density of a body by comparing its weight in air with its weight when submerged in water; and since he knew that gold was far more dense than brass, he had his solution.

When I was young I supposed that Archimedes' shout of triumph was in celebration of his own brilliance, and I rather think that my teachers put it that way, urging us to be scientists, with the implication "Wouldn't *you* like to make a discovery?" I know now, after having come across many scientists who have had the Eureka experience, that the cry "I have found it" has the emphasis on the word *found*, not on I. "I have *found* it!"

Now, my knowledge of Greek is not extensive, but as I read the lexicons, they indicate precisely this connotation of the word "eureka." It concerns a fortunate and unexpected discovery. Not "serendipity," mind you, not a lucky accident as by-product of a different search. Rather, it is the gift of heart's desire, something earnestly sought but wholly unattainable by one's own power of thought—something not earned but granted. I have never known a scientist who having had that experience of discovery was not made humble by it.

Vain scientists exist, to be sure—even Nobel Laureates. Adulation works a dangerous alchemy. But scientific vanity, I have observed, is most often attributable to the practitioners of what Thomas Kuhn (author of *The Structure of Scientific Revolutions*) calls "ordinary science." This kind of science follows established methods, often with great ingenuity, adding to the body of data with new levels of precision or details of analysis; it is consequently of quite practical importance. A good safe example for a scientist, I suppose, would be Tycho Brahe, the Danish astronomer of the sixteenth century, who built huge instruments—big but not essentially different from those already existing—in order to make precise measurements of the planets' motion. The precision of those measurements, as it turned out, was of enormous importance because those findings led Kepler to his model of elliptic orbits which, in turn, led to Newton's theory of gravity. But the measurements never gave Tycho himself any fundamental wisdom. Perhaps I do the old scoundrel an injustice; but he has always seemed to me a very vain man who did not know the meaning of gratitude and consequently was never granted the Eureka moment.

It is ordinary science that people generally admire—the man in the white lab coat, holding a test tube up to the light. Other disciplines are urged to imitate this ordinary science because of a belief in its efficiency. Jacques Barzun describes it: "In science the elements are clear, abstract, and unchangeable. . . . Because of this clarity and fixity, it is easy to use these concepts correctly; once their strange artificiality has been firmly grasped, it is then but the application of a method." Barzun decries its use as a paradigm for other disciplines and, indeed, one must agree with him.

Science increases mightily by the operation of its ordinary methods. The manipulation of techniques and the design of instruments are in themselves highly satisfying to the practitioner. There is a glamour to living on the frontier of knowledge, as scientists like to think they do, of extending what is known into new territory. It is satisfying—and tempting to vanity. But when I speak of the basis of science, it is not this ordinary science to which I refer, with its esoteric—even arcane—methodology. Not the systematic extension of frontiers constitutes the vital working of science but rather the sudden surprising leap, the jump to another plane. Kuhn calls these leaps "revolutions" in science, because they frequently move counter to established beliefs—outside the realm of methodology. And often they do change the situation of who's in charge, so to speak—Copernicanism superseding Ptolemaicism, atomicity winning over continuism, waves over particles, then in successive reversals theories of photons over waves. But to think of these insights, these moments of extraordinary science as revolutions is to indulge, I suspect, an intellectual's propensity for martyrdom, for seeing his heroes as beleaguered champions of truth opposing a powerful and benighted establishment. In all candor, scientists are hard put to it to find martyrs. Galileo lived to a ripe old age and never had his pension lifted, and the burning of Bruno was not for science. There *is* something heroic about the scientist in his total dedication to his discipline, his forgetfulness of his own

204 · UNBINDING PROMETHEUS

interests and well-being, but the most heroic thing about him is likely to be his wife, who has to put up with this strange, abstract, uncelibate monk of the modern world.

On his deathbed, Einstein, quite stoic about his own approaching end, was apparently troubled about what his devotion to physics had cost his wife. Was he wrong to pursue science with such single-minded abstraction? The habit of submission to a discipline nearly always *seems* selfish when one views it from the vantage point of normal human responsibilities and bonds. The psychologist Carl Jung has written of the creative person, "As a human being he may have moods and a will and personal aims," but in his work he is "man" in a higher sense—he is "collective man"—one who carries and shapes the life of mankind. "To perform this difficult office it is sometimes necessary for him to sacrifice happiness and everything that makes life worth living for the ordinary human being." It is not an easy path and yet not one that can be forsaken.

The novelist Henry James said that his characters came and beckoned to him, so that he was *forced* to write about them. The creative process costs the poet or the physicist or the artist an immense amount of his human energies; but the privilege of *seeing*, of being allowed to discover hidden relations, is the most prized reward he can receive. The writer speaks of his donné, his gift; and though the physicist does not call it that, he is nonetheless aware of it as something received, something which he is permitted to find, something for which he is responsible and for which he feels a deep, if inarticulate, gratitude.

Those creative leaps that we call revolutions in science are, more accurately, *revelations*. They are insights granted, not created or invented. Jacques Maritain, in speaking of creative intuition, remarks that "pure creation is not possible to man." He goes on: "Some inner content, received from elsewhere, is necessarily present." Art and poetry were Maritain's concern at the time, but his remark is equally applicable to physics. The nature of this received "inner content," this revelation, is worth some exploration.

It could be that Plato is up there kicking a hole in his realm of pure ideas, letting a little stream of ideal forms fall upon physicists. But I suspect physics is a good deal more Aristotelian than Platonic. Perhaps Coleridgean, maybe even—it hurts me to say—Wordsworthian, but not Platonic. Reality resides in the object. In perceiving the form of an object, we perceive its reality, not an analogue. True, we create models for the envisioned entities and invest them with all the information we have available. They then take on by their own volition a completeness, allowing new information to be drawn from them—information we ourselves did not previously provide. Now, being moderns, we can be skeptical about this mysterious tendency of a model to complete itself. Rather we might suppose that it draws from the culture out of which it comes certain principles of symmetry or resonances consistent with boundary conditions. Surely, says our skepticism, there is a natural explanation for its seemingly metaphysical manifestation. Perhaps so, but we can find an explanation only after making a discovery; we cannot anticipate, cannot predict something yet unknown. To complete a model ingeniously is to confine it to "ordinary science." For revelation to come, the scientist must be patient and let the model form itself in the imagination, "ignorant," as Sylvia Plath puts it, "of whatever angel may choose to flare/Suddenly at [one's] elbow."

Imagination, not fancy, is the pertinent faculty. I have always been skeptical of the anecdote about discovering the benzene molecule, in which Friedrich Kekulé, thoroughly fatigued from excessive striving in the laboratory, fell into a daydream in front of his fire, seeing little tongues of flame becoming phantasms of snakes dancing about, until they suddenly seized each other's tails and formed a closed ring.

According to the tale, our chemist came to himself and wrote down the carbon ring configuration for benzene. Perhaps the account is true; perhaps chemistry works in that strange sibylline manner. It is much like the story of the composition of "Kubla Khan," which despite my admiration of Coleridge has always aroused in me a bit of skepticism. Though the creative mind works cinematographically, it does not find its images by fancy, a free association of the surfaces of things. The dream sequence or the drug scene produces a semblance of creativity but is in reality only fanciful. When one tries keeping a notebook beside the bed for jotting down dreams, one is likely to have absolute drivel in the morning.

Imagination is different from fancy. It is not out of touch with the self, not out of communication and interchange with reality. The models formed in the imagination are not fantastic. They are symbolic, and, as Coleridge puts it, they "partake of the reality which they render intelligible." Imagination discovers images that in themselves have meaning for the reality involved. If the atom looks like a planetary system or a diagram of energy levels or mathematical function, these models speak quite directly to the phenomenon concerned. They are not similes: leprechauns, or kings and queens, or fuzzy little animals—or snakes. Nor are they apparitions or theophanies. They are generative images that come to the well-instructed imagination out of the matrix of reality.

Such patterns of discovery are fairly well established for creativity. First, a long period of intensive, exhausting study occurs in which solutions to a problem are sought by means that we could call ordinary—though few persons may be capable of attempting this ordinary procedure. In frustration and fatigue the mind retires from the problem for a time. Later, in a period of idleness, when the intellect is quiescent, suddenly a solution appears—usually an image but not always—with quite unexpected features. Despite its strangeness, the artist— if I may call the scientist that in this capacity—immediately recognizes its significance. There is a sudden snap of recognition; everything clicks into place. A peculiar certainty inheres in this recognition, an absolute confidence of its rectitude. Nothing in it speaks of the attitude, "Here's a good idea; let's try it out." Instead, a quiet satisfaction settles deep within this "artist," while on the surface a high excitement brings forth some expression of "Eureka."

Henri Poincaré recounts his long struggles with his Fuchsian functions—at first trying to prove that none such could exist, then forming with them a fairly elaborate series. Taking a needed break from his mathematical chores, he went with students on a geological exposition into the south of France, and there in a little village, as he was boarding a bus, he recalls, "At the moment when I put my foot on the step the idea came to me, without anything in my former thoughts seeming to have paved the way for it, that the transformations I had used to define the Fuchsian Functions were identical with those of non-Euclidean geometry." He paused only for a moment, then went on with his conversation with students, but he knew something important had been revealed to him. The revelation came to him, apparently, in the abstraction of an idea. Mathematicians are strange people. For most of us, in contrast, this experience comes as an image of some sort. I once asked Donald Kerst, the inventor of the Betatron, how his idea for that electron accelerator had emerged, and his story was much the same. Having worked long on the problem of particle acceleration, he was taking a vacation at LaJolla. He swam out in that beautiful bay to a rock and was there sunning himself, quite at ease with the world, when suddenly, without warning, the image of the moving magnetic field of a transformer came to him. He jumped from the rock, swam back, went to his room, and wrote down his insight. This pattern of creative intuition seems to be a general one. Poincaré testifies that there is a period of furious work before and another after, but the crucial moment is one of tranquility, of non-volition.

Most of us surely have these moments. Yet I have known brilliant people who could not submit to them, could not forgo the self, and therefore never accomplished works of true originality.

I want to fasten on these moments of submission for a few minutes. Perhaps they are not Wordsworthian after all. The experience is not the overflow of powerful emotions recollected in tranquility. It is not that active. A kind of melding with being occurs. And I suspect this melding is a pre-condition for gratitude. Already, before any gift is given, an acceptance is on hand. Now let me not make preposterous claims; I shall not maintain that the revelations of which I speak are miracles. They are quite readily explainable in natural terms. The material for them has come out of the cultural environment and out of the personal history of the thinker; and the act of submission has so reduced the barriers between concepts that moderately free association takes place. In it the quasi-active mind recognizes and stabilizes the particular associations which have significance. This is a more sensible explanation for a scientist to make than any resort to angelic visitations. And surely one can be as grateful for such a condition to come about as one would be for miracles. But, for the sake of economy, let me go on with my figure.

Miracles do not happen on demand. Maybe they could occur in this manner for Moses, but if I remember correctly he paid a dear price for his presumption. Miracles are gifts, and the conditions for gratitude are already present when the gift is given. Gratitude tempers the shout of Eureka and couples with humility to place the stress on the right word of the translation. "I've found it!"

There is something paradoxical in thus recognizing gratitude as the basis of physics. Physics, I have said, is a very masculine subject, and gratitude is a difficult virtue for the male to assume. I grew up with my father's grace at table saying "Teach us to be humble and grateful" and recognized early how rarely we achieve those conditions. In all likelihood it is pre-conditions for humility and gratitude that we fail at—a melding with reality, a rise to tranquility—what the poet Keats called "negative capability."

Despite the masculine difficulty, science has erected a structure of notable magnificence—partly, it is true, in praise of man, but, chiefly, one must declare, in praise of God. How complete, we might wonder, is this structure? How far do we have to go? Are the opportunities infinite? Or are they, like the earth's treasure, finite and irreplaceable? There was a time at the turn of the last century when the physicist Michelson said "Science is complete. From now on, it is a matter of fixing the decimal point." The splendid achievement of Maxwell's Equations had united electricity and magnetism and fused them into radio waves, of which light was seen to be the acme and the glory. Everything, it seemed would ultimately reside in these equations. But Michelson himself conducted the crucial experiment which led Einstein to relativity, both restoring man to the center of the universe and removing him from the godhead. Max Planck, about the same time, found that beautifully continuous electromagnetic world to be discrete and particular. On these two discoveries, physics opened to a new and vigorous three-score and ten years. Now, I think it likely that the universe of ideas is, indeed, finite but that we are far from exhausting it. We may be nearing the end of our Promethean push for elementary particles—that is, having observed the fleeting j particles and postulated the quarks, charmed and in colors, we have almost reached the limits of our ability to give substance to images. This push from atoms to nucleons to neutrons and protons to whole families of hadrons and leptons and on to quarks has been in essence, for all the new ideas required, an expansion of the frontiers opened a life-span ago. We may be near the edge.

But there will come a new tranquility, a new gift, a new occasion for gratitude. That constant submission to a generosity outside the self is the very essence of science, and, I suspect, of existence as we know it.

16

The Economics of Taste

WHAT IS IT that causes a buyer to choose one item over another? that makes social interaction easy and gracious and transforms business or professional meetings into pleasant occasions, much like social events? What is it that makes a display or an advertisement effective? that makes a property have high occupancy and long standing?

If I should say that the answer to these questions is univocally and unambiguously taste, I would no doubt be considerably overstating the case. The brute components of the marketplace are more powerful determinants. But, when the economic factors are near the balance point, as they generally are, then indeed taste does enter into the arena of judgment. Financial advantage represents the apparent, perhaps superficial, economic effects of taste. The deeper-lying, more pervasive operations are closer to the heart of culture and worth one's careful scrutiny.

Taste is a dangerous thing to discuss. Nothing so arouses indignation as for someone to presume to specify standards for taste. The part of caution demands that these be left wholly relative, with one person's preference considered as good as another's—one man's meat and so on. But caution lies next to cowardice; I shall adopt no such stance. The classic position, I believe, was assumed two centuries ago by Samuel Johnson in a remark to the fluttering dowager who sought to modify his acerbic judgments. "But Dr. Johnson," she protested, "It's all a matter of taste." His unrelenting reply was, "Yes, madam. Good taste and bad taste."

Though I agree with Dr. Johnson, the definition of taste I shall presently assay will probably be disappointingly mild. It should incite no riots. There will be nothing absolute about it, even though I do mean to imply in it standards for judgment. I undertake it with awareness of its naïveté, knowing full well that between the genuine taste of simple folk and the cultivated taste of the most sophisticated stretches a vast wasteland of mediocrity, where taste declines from poor to bad to perverse. I am well aware that popular taste is generally bad and that what makes it bad is what makes it popular —and, further, that this social defect is many times callously exploited for commercial gain or political advantage. I know that many in society, pledged to brutishness, are offended by good taste and feel a duty to attack it as hypocrisy or affectation. But I want to be as innocent as possible of all this knowledge. I shall select no whipping boys, place no blame on television or billboards, castigate no tycoons, journalists, or ad men. My mode will be analytical, not prophetic, with the aim of seeing the social structure in its relation to taste. For taste is more than a decoration upon society; it is one of its sources of energy and its primary instrument of decision.

Taste is an inner response of recognition, to the effect that a particular action or object in society is genuine in itself and fitting for the situation in which it participates. Fitness implies a measure of quality that serves as a shared standard for society. Accordingly, taste is a social necessity rather than a private indulgence.

Artists and taste are not bedfellows, not at least in a generative sense. Taste cohabits with the audience instead of with the artist. An artist is impregnated with something much more profound than taste, something more archetypal, robust, and brutal. And, if what is produced by that union is a true art piece, then taste, though jarred and insulted, redefines itself to encompass the new revelation. We need only recall the furore that greeted Beethoven's symphonies or Marcel Duchamp's nude at the Armory show to recognize this intimate interchange between artist and audience. What it says to us is that art is indeed a social operation, that the artist, though working apart from the community, still is wholly within it. He speaks to society, corrects it, alters it by calling it toward something nearer to what it is supposed to be. What art alters in society is taste.

Taste, then, is not the inner vision of the artist, nor that strange and wonderful faculty in the viewer that recognizes the essence of an art piece from any era, wherever it occurs, in any medium—poetry, drama, music, painting, sculpture— what I can only call its truth, quite independent of any consideration other than the piece itself. This faculty is innate, in principle universally present in every human being, but in practice lying dormant in almost all, suppressed by a fear of certainty. So rare are those who maintain this ability to recognize firsthand the truth of an art piece that they are indeed, as Arnold Bennett called them, the "passionate few." Out of the flurry of temporal styles and smartness that make a figure popular in its time, they winnow those sempiternal agents of revelation for the human spirit—Homer, Sophocles, Phidias, Michelangelo, Shakespeare, El Greco, Beethoven, Dostoevsky, Faulkner, and of course many others. And though a Melville dies in obscurity, these passionate few keep the white whale alive.

Taste is no more the ability to recognize the absolute than it is the engendering genius of the artist. Taste is social, not universal. Nor should we go with Immanuel Kant in letting taste be the ability to recognize beauty and to render an *a priori* judgment that something is indeed beautiful. Taste is aesthetic, though it does not require beauty as its object. We might borrow from Kant, however, his definition of taste as a "faculty to choose in agreement with others that which sensitively pleases." Too mild for beauty, I say, but fine for taste.

If taste is a social phenomenon, it can be discerned accurately only if one is aware of the distinct strata of society. Let me use as an aid for the moment Daniel Bell's schema set forth in *The Cultural Contradictions of Capitalism*; he sees three components in contemporary society: the techno-economic, the polity, and the culture. Taste, I would say, governs culture, the realm of the symbolic, as Bell puts it. For him, in its formal aspects, this realm is "the arena of expressive symbolism: those efforts, in painting, poetry, and fiction, or within the religious forms of litany, liturgy, and ritual, which seek to explore and express the meanings of human existence in some imaginative form." These meanings, he would have it, stem from the existential agonies which confront human beings through all time, "how one meets death, the nature of tragedy and the character of heroism, the definition of loyalty and obligation, the redemption of the soul, the meaning of love and sacrifice, the understanding of compassion, the tension between an animal and a human nature, the claims of instinct and restraint." In a larger context than art and ritual, I would add not only other arts but folkways and events and would append to his litany of agonies a brighter listing of those instances of interaction that yield pleasure: breaking bread together, celebrating, playing, communing. Of course the artist is in the culture—very prominently so— but he goes his own way and is essentially ungovernable. The operating governor of culture, as I see it, then, is taste, that faculty of sensing what is most apt and good (and therefore fundamentally satisfying) in the society in which it operates.

The techno-economic sphere is in radical disjunction from culture. What Bell calls its axial principle is functional rationality, whose regulating mode is economizing; its terms are efficiency, least cost, greatest return, maximization, optimization, productivity. The structure is bureaucratic and hierarchical. Authority rests less in person than in position. "And indeed," he says, "a person becomes an object or a thing in this portion of society." Taste, seemingly, would enter this realm only insofar as it affects the market for the goods and services produced.

The other component, the polity, is the arena of social justice and power, exercised in conformity with a society's tradition. The axial principle in a democratic society is governance by the consent of the governed. The implicit condition is the equality of all persons. The method is by representation, and, though administration is bureaucratic, management is by bargaining or by law. But because the polity operates by tradition (the persistent residue of culture), it is not in so marked disjunction with culture as is the economic segment.

It is the business of civic and cultural organizations to discover and nurture the bonds that link the three separate strata into a unity. The three segments are readily recognized. They are highly institutionalized as industries, governments, and non-profit enterprises—universities, hospitals, symphonies, museums, and countless other groupings, among which I should place the most fundamental of institutions, the home. Peter Drucker, in his latest book, sticks a tentative toe into the non-profit pool of management and pronounces it much the more complex of the three. "There is no adequate study of it," he says. When industrialists try to solve the problems of cultural institutions by technocratic means (I am paraphrasing Bell) or when representatives of the polity seek to alter non-profit organizations by political procedures, they are naïve and misguided, however high-minded they may be. In this prime segment, culture, different purposes prevail and different ends are sought; and therefore (I would go on to say) governance by boards and even by administration is largely fictional. Like Crispin's Crispin, the dog who belonged to himself, these institutions belong to their purposes and are directed by them. Seemingly they submit to no adequate measure of success or failure. Free of the profit motive, they are incredibly durable, and many of them long outlive their mission. They are invested in tradition and can draw against their inheritance.

An adequate study of management for non-profit institutions would involve a rethinking of economics in terms appropriate to the ends sought. Economics, in its root meaning the management of the household, the *oikos*, is the management of resources in the production of value. In this context, one can assume that taste has value: its enhancement makes life more valuable than it otherwise is—"happier," we could say, in an Aristotelian sense, where every experience, our griefs and existential agonies included, become fraught with meaning and intensely real. In a paradoxical way, things become more real as they become more symbolic. This transformation accounts for the genuine expressions of art, as well as for the conventionalized patterns that deeply satisfy us in our communal existence—a carefully printed book, a well-appointed room, a precisely run ceremony, a definitive performance of a symphony, a sensitive interpretation of a drama, good food, good fellowship. The world becomes a better place not only as such patterns multiply but as the faculty of appreciating them becomes more widespread. These cultural "goods" are the stuff of existence toward which all other activities tend and to which they are in service. The "economics" of taste, we can say, is the management of resources—our lives—in the enhancement of value, the cultural "goods."

How does taste grow and spread? First of all by the presence of good design. The designer, unlike the artist, is the direct agent of the public and hence must guide and fashion, giving the best possible form to current public desires. Taste reinvests in itself, so to say. Design generates the concept of design in its observers. Unlike the money economy, taste in-creases value by plenitude, not scarcity. The more taste there is, the better the market for it. Therein lies one of the dangers associated with taste, however—a tendency to imitate the externals of design instead of the concept. Genuine taste has about it a unique quality, much as art has, involving the selection and appreciation of things in their particular situations exhibiting their own intentions. Without this concept, an imitation of taste is likely to lead to bad taste or to none at all. Style, now, is easier to imitate and fortunately is much more perishable, like fads in clothes or the names of little girls. In economic terms, on the other hand, taste is a durable good, like refrigerators or buildings. It is true that style directs the design of buildings, but if taste guides style the building remains an aesthetic asset long after style has gone its way.

The arts and their criticism are another ongoing invest-ment for culture. Critics, in that they write for newspapers and journals, keep in motion a constant conversation about the arts, playing an important part in adult education. Their acceptance of professional responsibility for evaluating arti-facts and performances is a necessary accompaniment to the arts. The function of criticism is not so much to pronounce as to stimulate reflection, to awaken an inner action of taste. Likes and dislikes frequently lead one astray—through senti-mentality, familiarity, or other considerations irrelevant to the judgment at hand. The critic calls one to look back into imagination for a second and more dispassionate seeing of af-fairs. The act of reflection instructs the taste.

But even more than design and the arts, education is the chief disseminator of aesthetic sensibility. Society has turned over to schools the development of children's taste, just as it has assigned to education the development of their character. For the child, music is of prime importance. The play and then the joy of music establishes a foundation in the early grades; and at the secondary level, a group experience in chorus or orchestra, under a demanding director whose taste is impeccable in catalogue and performance, invests students with an intuitive non-verbal critical sense that serves as paradigm for all later expressive experience. Beyond the high-school years, the importance of music as a formative experience diminishes, whereas the visual arts and poetry flower in the person much later because the aesthetic of these arts has philosophic dimensions and obvious analogical references.

In my own scheme of things college education is based upon the fundamental apparatus of criticism, whose paradigm is literature. The experience of understanding a complex work of literary art opens the mind to a new level of consciousness wherein all learning becomes available, once the process of transforming information into knowledge is mastered. Taste is the guide that presents an object to philosophic speculation, wherein the two modes of knowing—rational and aesthetic—conjoin in judgment. That general pattern makes up the critical act around which all the skill and content of learning in any discipline cluster, be it physics or art, economics or theology.

Education as we know it is largely a ward of the state, operated primarily to service the economy in its needs and incidentally to produce good citizens. Certainly at the elementary and secondary levels, education belongs to the polity and has utilitarian purposes. Yet, in truth, education is an activity of culture and has as its chief though often forgotten end the perpetuation and revitalization of culture. The services it renders to the political and economic realms are by-products. What is sought from the schools as product, whether society knows it or not, is a constant flow of young persons whose desires lead to an understanding of social issues and participation in them, with a consequent development of enabling skills. That participation—and enjoyment—is partly economic, partly civic, but wholly cultural. Obviously I mean culture in its broad sense of being the life of a people, expressed, most often unconsciously, in symbolic forms of feasting, celebration, and play. If educators could watch young basketball players at their incessant practice on the playground, they would immediately apprehend the principle that skills follow desires. The exemplum holds for any skill, even the most intellectual. The fallacy of "back to basics" lies in the belief that drill in itself, without *eros*, accomplishes learning. What a curriculum must do is awaken desire and a guiding taste for symbolic experience—such as reading and calculating. All of us, educators included, are so conditioned by functional rationalism that when we are put in any post of authority, our references immediately become efficiency, completeness, or productivity, borrowed from the techno-economic realm. We forget the purpose of education. We fail to remember that we are engendering pleasure as the inner instructor, the young person's self-instructor for life. It is not that we should set out to make learning entertainment; learning is hard work. But we must make it important and full of an appropriate joy. And for child or grown-up, to work hard at something important is in itself to know pleasure.

If there is such a thing as productivity in education—and I suspect there is—it is in this sort of value-added per effort-expended that it must be measured. I want to grant the importance of the concept of productivity, which, one must remember, is the number of units of goods produced per man-hour of labor. In the industrial world, a gain in productivity is the chief element that allows an increase in individual income without inflation—that is, in the national product (or GNP) per person. Our state of affluence is a reflection of productivity. Our ability to compete in the world market depends on a high productivity. This measure is an important index to our economic health. Yet productivity is somewhat ambiguous and difficult to assess even in the industrial world. As an example, what happens when an electronic wristwatch replaces a mechanical one? Is it simply counted on the production scale, unit for unit, with the one replaced? The electronic watch is far more precise, far more reliable, and far more versatile in functions performed. The inexpensive one on my wrist, now several years old, keeps time within seconds per year, tells me the day of the week, is a stop-watch accurate to tenths of a second, and plays "The Yellow Rose of Texas." Obviously it is much more valuable than the old kind; but its price hardly tells us so. The inflation-adjusted equivalent to the dollar that I spent as a boy for a clumsy pocket watch will now buy a good electronic timepiece. The added utility is not given credit as invested value as long as the adjusted price remains the same.

In moving to the second realm of which we have spoken, the polity, we can readily see the complexity of any such measure as productivity and the difficulty of applying it to realms other than the economic. It can hardly be the number of laws passed per legislator or regulations issued per bureaucrat. Some other acceptable social scale of value is needed.

And when we speak of the non-profit sphere, the problem is even more complicated. Gains in productivity in the industrial realm are brought about by better production tools, by making a greater investment per worker in equipment. The investment per worker in the solid-state electronic industry now stands at $50,000, so *Time* magazine reported recently. Concerning an enterprise as labor intensive as education— something like eighty percent of scholastic expenditures goes for salaries and wages—an industrialist immediately thinks in terms of equipment, of capital goods replacing labor. Hence the enthusiasm a few years back for teaching machines and computer-assisted instruction. The supposition was that through such mechanical means costs could be drastically cut. In fact, they could not, but that misapprehension is not the point. When I revealed to an industrialist friend the results of a study demonstrating that, with any teaching machine, under any reasonable assumptions, the costs of education would rise, he was nonetheless certain that the change should still be made. He was right, of course, if, as he presumed, education is part of the service sector of a techno-economic system. The consideration in that area is not reduced costs but reduced manpower. Any labor released could go elsewhere and be similarly productive, it is assumed, with the transfer increasing the national effort. "Education," he said, "is a drag on the economy."

This is a serious charge. Are educators guilty of so heinous a crime? If so, they are not alone. The entire non-profit sphere operates in the same way. One must applaud the use of instrumentation in hospitals, but it quite certainly has not reduced costs. Neither has it increased productivity in terms of patient-care-delivered per man-hour-spent. Now the end purpose of hospitals is not medical services delivered but the health of the community. In the ideal extreme of total health, the hospital's productivity drops to zero. If, in contrast, affluence were measured in units of health, a different sort of index would apply.

Let me back away, however, from outlawing the application of productivity to health, education, and welfare, to symphonies, museums, the performing arts generally, and to all symbolic expressions in their creation and display. The situation is that each of us is an inhabitant of all three realms of society. Each of the three realms spans the entire society, and each provides a vantage point from which to evaluate, in its own terms, the worth of society. Moreover, actual participation in one realm involves rewards in another. Within the economic realm, for example, culture has one of its major components, the joy of work; and any cultural measurement must include this economic activity within its own satisfaction index. Further, the industrial sector benefits immensely from the output of the other realms in their work toward a healthy, happy, intelligent population, an orderly society, and a receptive market. There should be some way of taking into account gains in the enterprises devoted to those ends— of expressing productivity in value terms appropriate to purposes and then assigning a coupling coefficient. But seemingly the best that can be done in this direction is to let cost reflect value and by such a stratagem to neutralize gains or losses in these "non-productive" realms—to consider them a drag, so to say, diluting the gains that industry brings about. For this reason the federal bureau of statistics deletes most of the governmental and non-profit contributions to the GNP in figuring productivity; otherwise the calculated measure would be reduced by more than twenty percent. Contrariwise, whatever measures truly apply to culture or to the polity must accept the drag of the other two realms.

To put it positively, each of the realms is in service to the others. The affluence of the economy in monetary terms elevates the other two to greater output—what might be called affluence—in their terms. Similarly for cultural and civic endeavors; when one of the members seeks to divest itself of this drag, it harms the whole body. I suspect there really is a danger to the culture and to the polity in the great multinational corporations. The hugeness of the enterprises and the blackmail of affluence invest them with an overriding power that weighs upon the polity, endangering a free society. The facelessness of ownership and the incessant growth of system enslaves individuals and robs them of their hard-won pleasure in work. And yet the very greed, we might call it, of the Cyclopean corporations drives them toward the emancipation of their captives through automation and the use of robots. An apparent drawback could become a boon.

The danger, then, lies not so much in industry *per se* as in a failure of the other two realms to make equivalent gains in their own terms. Not that the apparatus of government should increase. Quite the contrary. The very success in equality, in equitable distribution of justice in the general welfare, should reduce the apparatus needed for social aid and release persons from the tedium of bureaucratic work. The cultural realm, in the end, is the crucial element. To what purpose are the successes of economy and government if not directed toward the satisfaction of higher desires—not an inordinate indulgence in amusement and diversion but a participation in the symbolic expressiveness that the human person discovers in communion with others. Largely, I would say, this expressiveness is to be found in a committed work, wherein one gains a livelihood in an enterprise that in some way furthers the aims of the entire society.

A city's investment in education, design, criticism, and the arts yields a return in taste. And taste, the governor of culture, makes a community rich in the shared goods that bond it together in happiness, giving a city its unique character and destiny. Taste guides us in many of our most important activities, enabling us to choose that which is the highest possible good and at the same time most fit and pleasing to the community. Like a gustatory sensation, taste must give flavor and depth to the lives of people. What I would urge is no new Eden, no paradise on earth. Those old existential agonies are ever with us. We shall all taste pain and anguish, witness death, and come to it ourselves. But these seeming diminishments, too, can take on a full-bodied and satisfying flavor. As Keats writes, in his "Ode on Melancholy," only the cultivated appetite can experience either joy or anguish. And, pursued to their source, these two apparent opposites spring from the same origin:

> Ay, in the very temple of Delight
> Veil'd Melancholy has her sovran shrine,
>   Though seen of none save him whose strenuous tongue
> Can burst Joy's grape against his palate fine. . . .

The disciplined taste alone can experience joy fully ("burst Joy's grape"), can enter into the shrine of "veil'd Melancholy." In the end, taste is our way of experiencing life with zest, of feasting upon reality and finding it deeply pleasing.

Index

Achilles 136
Aeschylus 1, 15, 21-23, 30, 34, 151
alchemy 38, 64, 139, 183, 202
America 4, 11-13, 29, 81, 135, 143, 151, 186
analysis 3, 45, 65, 74, 85, 86, 89-91 124, 128, 129, 130, 155, 179, 202
angel 36, 62, 85, 89, 118, 163, 168 193-195, 198, 199, 208
applied science 154, 155, 164-166
Aquinas, Thomas 193, 194
archetype 4, 34, 36, 162, 212
Archimedes 72, 80, 201
Ariel 52, 53, 56-59, 61-65
Aristotle 30, 41, 77, 91, 92, 121, 136, 155, 182, 205, 216
astrology 5, 38, 52
atom 44, 120, 159, 160, 162, 171-173, 176, 192, 206

Bachelard, Gaston 87, 93, 161, 168
Bacon, Francis 6, 34
Bacon, Roger 37
Baconian 47
Barzun, Jacques 50, 195-199, 203
baseball 30
Bell, Daniel 166, 214, 215
Bennett, Arnold 213
Bible 135
biotechnology 166, 167
black magic 40, 43, 57, 58
Bohr, Niehls 120, 159-162, 192
Bose-Einstein 189
Brahe, Tycho 5, 6, 186, 187, 202
Bronowski, Jacob 34, 39, 40
Brownian movement 191

calculus 100, 119
Caliban 52-54, 56-63
Camp, Walter 28
Cartwright, Alexander Jay 29
Castro, Joao de 181
catastrophe vii, 14, 18
charm 200
chemistry 8, 168, 192, 206
child 2, 37, 59, 73, 82, 94, 97-99, 168, 178, 179, 201, 217, 219
Chiron 25, 33
Christ 24, 42, 52, 63, 90, 91

Christian 33, 75, 134, 154, 170-172
Christianity 82, 154
civilization 9, 16, 21, 22, 24, 26, 31, 60, 81, 103, 121, 134, 169, 174, 179,
Coleridge, Samuel Taylor 87, 104, 105, 109, 205, 206
college vii, 14, 16, 32, 53, 57, 96, 97, 100, 132, 134, 136, 139, 143, 146, 218
Commedia 36, 37
computer 28, 107, 114, 115, 146, 157, 165, 167, 175, 220
conjugate variables 119, 121, 122, 125
conservation principle 171, 195
Copernicus 38-39, 160, 182, 203
cosmos 11, 101, 102, 129
creative 11, 23, 53, 61, 67, 85, 89, 99, 105, 112, 115, 116, 155, 170, 204, 206, 207
crisis 14, 16, 17, 21, 100
criticism 74, 81, 84, 91, 116, 129, 161, 217, 218, 223
Crombie, A. C. 180, 181
culture vii, ix, 1, 4, 9-12, 22, 31, 46, 47, 50, 61, 67, 72, 102, 116, 121, 129, 154-156, 161, 162, 168, 169, 169-171, 191, 195, 205, 211, 214, 215, 217, 218, 221-223
curriculum vii, viii, 16, 76, 95-97, 130, 135, 138, 144-146, 219
Cymbeline 105

Dante 36, 37, 87, 95, 129, 193
Digges, Leonard 186
Dionysius 193
Dionysus 17
discipline 39, 48, 49, 50, 51, 55, 72, 80, 81, 86, 88, 89, 137-139, 146, 147, 168, 188, 190, 197, 199, 200, 203, 204, 218
Divine Comedy 36
Dostoevsky, Fyodor 31, 213
Drucker, Peter 215
Duchamp, Marcel 213

education vii, x, 1, 3, 11, 15, 16, 21, 32, 33, 41, 49, 50, 52-54, 57, 58, 63-65, 67, 72, 74-82, 84, 85, 92, 93-99, 101, 103, 116, 117, 118, 123-129, 131, 132-141, 143, 144, 217-221, 223
energy 110, 111, 114

Einstein, Albert 72, 110, 111, 114, 120, 121, 126, 128, 130, 159, 161, 189-191, 204, 209
electromagnetic 28, 160, 173, 189, 209
electrons 120, 159, 160, 189,
Eliot, T.S. 87, 94, 95, 109, 134
energy 8, 12, 17, 26, 28, 74, 119-122, 125-127, 130, 152, 160, 169, 171-179, 205, 212
equality 12-13, 97, 129-131, 153, 215, 222
equilibrium 12,, 14, 16, 25, 32
Euclid 88
eureka 201, 202, 207, 208
Everyman 35, 36
extraordinary science 165, 197, 203

fancy 58, 66, 104, 105, 166, 205, 206
fantasy 11, 25, 49
Faulkner, William 102, 122, 136, 153, 154, 213
Faust 33-36, 42-44, 46-49, 62, 153, 154, 158
Faustbuch 34, 36,
Faustus 34-36, 38-43, 49, 57, 58, 152, 153
Ferdinand 54, 55, 57, 59, 61, 63, 65, 129, 147
Fermi, Enrico 173, 189, 191
Fermi-Dirac 189
Ficino, Marsilio 57
first moment, of learning 85, 86, 89
fission 28, 44, 47, 173, 176, 177, 191
football 29, 145
forbidden knowledge 24, 33, 36, 153, 155
Frost, Robert 116
Fuchsian functions 207
fusion 28, 84, 174, 176, 177

Galileo 6, 39, 72, 160, 170, 180-182, 186, 187, 203
Gell-Mann 130
Geoffrey of Beaux 183
Goethe, Johann Wolfgang 43, 153
gratitude 201, 202, 204, 208-210
Greeks 30, 33, 64, 80, 85, 134, 136, 159, 198, 201, 202, 204, 208-210
Grosseteste, Robert 181
GUT 130, 131

Heisenberg, Werner 112, 120, 121, 159-162, 199

Herakles 11, 26, 33
Hiroshima 44
Holbein, Hans 184-186
Holton, Gerald 191, 192, 194, 200
Hopkins, Gerard Manley 89

image 10, 11, 17, 24, 46, 57, 64, 74, 78, 86, 87, 89, 91, 92, 98, 99, 101, 105, 111-112, 114, 136, 138, 158 159, 161, 162, 164, 165, 183, 187, 206, 207, 209,
imagination 4, 9, 11, 15, 22-26, 32, 33, 36, 46 50, 52, 62-67,, 74, 76, 78, 79, 82,86, 87, 89, 91, 97-101, 104-110, 112-17, 121-124, 131, 135, 136, 138, 151, 153, 157-159, 161-169, 173, 183, 190-193, 196, 198, 205, 206, 217
independent colleges 140, 141
industrialism 98, 157, 168
industry 13, 28, 106, 144, 151, 166, 167, 220, 222
innovation 3, 13, 21, 28, 30, 105, 115, 173, 190
Inquisition 39
insight 51, 75, 78, 82, 86, 90, 91, 118, 120, 127, 162, 164, 166, 168, 207

James, Henry 30, 135, 171, 204
Johnson, Samuel 211, 212
Joule, James 171
Joyce, James 131
Jung, Carl 204

Kant, Immanuel 213, 214
Keats, John 108, 209, 223
Kekulé, Friedrich 205
Kepler, Johannes 6, 39, 181, 183, 187, 202
Kerst, Donald 207
kinetic 125, 191, 192
King Lear 53, 136
Kubla Khan 206
Kuhn, Thomas 162-164, 197, 202, 203

learning vii, 3, 15, 16, 36, 37, 41, 48, 50, 52, 54, 55, 57, 58, 63-65, 67, 70, 84, 85, 88, 92, 93-96, 99, 100, 102, 104, 109, 113, 114, 116, 123-127, 131, 134, 135, 137, 139, 140, 155, 169, 182
Leibnitz, G. W. 172
Leonardo da Vinci 185
Levin, Harry 33

liberal education 11, 32,, 41, 51, 72, 74-76, 79, 80, 81, 82, 84, 93, 94, 97, 99, 101, 103, 116, 117, 132, 135, 137-141, 155
Lindsay, Robert 181
literature x, 72, 75, 99, 105, 131, 135, 138, 193, 218

McLuhan, Marshall 113
Macbeth 53
magic 39, 40, 42, 43, 47, 50-53, 56-58, 61-64, 66, 131, 152
Mann, Thomas 2, 130
mapping 87-92, 111, 192
Maritain, Jacques 65, 74, 80, 204
Marlowe, Christopher 34, 35, 39, 41, 57, 58, 152, 153
Maxwell, James Clark 173, 190, 192, 209
measurement 5, 120, 181-183, 185-187, 195, 221
medicine 38, 41, 139, 157, 158, 165, 167, 221
medieval 31, 34-36, 38, 57, 65, 192
Meitner, Lisa 44, 173
Melville, Herman 213
Mephistophilis 40, 42, 62, 152
Merchant of Venice 55, 104
Meredith, George 122
Mertonian Rule 181
metaphor 4, 39, 58, 89, 109, 118, 119, 124, 126, 137, 160
Michelson-Morley 189
Middle Ages 9, 12, 33, 36, 38, 162, 182, 187
Midsummer Night's Dream 60, 123
Millay, Edna St. Vincent 88
Milton, John 147, 193, 194
model 73, 74, 86, 87, 111, 141, 151, 159-162, 164, 169, 174, 190-192, 197, 198, 200, 202, 205
Molière, Jean Baptiste 7
momentum 119-121, 125, 126, 171, 172
Moses 122, 136, 154, 208
myth viii, 4, 7-9, 12, 23-26, 33, 34, 43, 46, 47, 49, 50, 60, 102, 113, 120, 129, 141, 152, 153, 158, 170, 174, 175, 180, 195; of creation 129; of equality 12; of fact 4-8, 8, 10, 16, 195

neutrino 172
new age x, 1, 3, 9-11, 13, 14, 21, 26, 32, 67, 158, 162

Newman, John Henry 75-77, 79-81, 116, 135, 155
Newton, Isaac 72, 128, 161, 180, 190, 202

Odysseus 136
Oedipus at Colonus 63
"oh" moment 86
Olbert of Saxony 181
Olympians 23, 25, 136
Oppenheimer, J. Robert 44
ordinary science 197, 202, 203, 205
Ortega y Gasset, José 133, 195-199

Paideia Program 95, 96
paradigm 50, 164, 197, 199, 203, 218
particle 120, 121, 129, 161, 172, 189, 207
Pericles 53
photon 159-161, 189
physics x, 8, 10, 43, 72, 84, 86, 88, 105, 120, 121, 129-131, 147, 159, 168, 172, 173, 180-182, 188, 190, 191, 196-200, 204, 205, 208, 209, 218
Pico della Mirandola 57
Pius XII 193
Planck, Max 8, 105, 120-122, 128, 159, 160, 173, 176, 190, 209
Planck's constant 8, 120-122, 128, 160, 190
plastic 157, 169
Plath, Sylvia 205
Plato vii, 72, 136, 105,
poem 36, 66, 89-91, 147, 190
poiesis 11, 67, 91, 101, 154,
Poincaré 159, 207
politics 2, 12, 14, 16, 31, 32, 41, 45, 46, 48, 53, 75, 76, 136, 148, 176, 21, 215, 218
probability 8, 10, 44, 118, 174, 175, 194
productivity 13, 116, 140, 151, 178, 215, 219-222
professors viii, ix, 2, 3, 78
Prometheus 1, 2, 3, 15, 21-26, 31, 33, 34, 46, 49, 60, 63, 151-156, 158, 169, 209
Prospero 43, 50-63, 65-67
Ptolemaic system 203
pure science 154, 155, 164, 166
Pythagoras 45

quantitative 48, 65, 99, 100, 129, 180-182
quantum 120, 160, 161, 173, 176, 189, 192, 199, 200
quarks 10, 120, 131, 200, 209

Reardon, B. M. G. 195
recognition viii, 54, 55, 71, 85, 86, 89, 107, 113, 162, 164, 166, 167, 181, 186, 196, 207, 212
redundancy 104-108, 110, 116, 117
revolution 2, 21, 32, 39

St. Paul 136
St. Augustine 136
Sarton, George 180
Scholasticism 172, 182, 187, 220
schools vii, 18, 65, 95-99, 103, 132, 136, 140, 141, 217, 218
Schrödinger, Erwin 161, 162, 199
science ix, 1, 6-8, 10, 11, 33-35, 37-41, 43, 44, 46-49, 50, 51, 57, 64, 66, 67, 72, 75, 80, 81, 98, 100, 112, 129, 137, 154-156, 161, 164-168, 170-173, 175, 180, 181, 187, 188, 190, 195-197, 200, 201-205, 209, 210
scientist 6, 16, 37, 43, 48, 50, 51, 57, 155, 162-166, 193, 196, 202, 203, 205, 206, 208
Scotus, Duns 172
second moment, of learning 89
senses 8, 15, 79, 97, 108-118, 158
Serres, Michel 169
Shakespeare 6, 50, 52-54, 57, 58, 60, 66, 72
Smith, Cyril 184
Snopes, Flem 136
solar 38, 159, 160, 177
Soto, Domenico 182
sound 1, 32, 41, 65, 85, 89, 109, 110, 158
speech viii, ix, x, 60, 62, 112, 124
stability 9, 12, 21, 25, 28, 31
state schools 140, 141
Steven, Simon 180, 183
Stevens, Gavin 136
students viii, 2, 16, 42, 48, 53, 86, 96, 100,124, 132-134, 139, 144, 207, 218

style 12, 28, 81, 107, 108, 129, 139, 178, 191, 192, 199, 217
Suarez, Francisco 194
symbol viii, 21, 24, 43, 53, 56, 64, 84, 123, 124, 174, 206, 214, 216, 219, 221, 223

taste 108-110, 132, 133, 158, 168, 211-219, 223
teacher viii, 3, 7, 76, 124, 202
techné 15, 21, 34, 46, 49, 151, 152, 158
technology ix, 1, 11, 21, 22, 28, 30, 31, 33, 40, 42, 44, 46, 47, 49, 50-52, 67, 100, 105, 106, 115, 151-158, 165, 167-169, 170, 175, 176, 178, 179, 181
Tempest 43, 50, 52-55, 57, 63-66
theoretical physics 8, 181, 182
theoria 91, 92
Theseus 63
third moment, of learning 88
Thomas (Aquinas) ix, x, 2, 162, 172, 193, 194, 197, 200, 202
Thorndike, Lynn 180
Titan 21-24, 136, 156
TOE 131, 215
Turner, Frederick W. 64
Twelfth Night 53

Ulysses 37
Uncertainty 7, 8, 112, 118-122, 131, 173, 175, 191
utilitarianism 75, 132

vector 125, 126
Vernier, Pierre 6, 185, 186
Virgil 36

Waldseemuller, Martin 186
Warren, Robert Penn 71, 93-94
wave 8, 10, 109, 116, 161, 192
wavelength 120, 121
white magic 40, 51, 57, 58, 62, 66
Whitehead, Alfred North 182
Wordsworth, William 95, 205, 208

Yahweh 136
Yeats, William Butler 162
Zeus 15, 21-23, 25, 26, 31, 33, 49, 151, 152, 156, 158